# NEWCOMER'S™
# HANDBOOK

### FOR

# Chicago

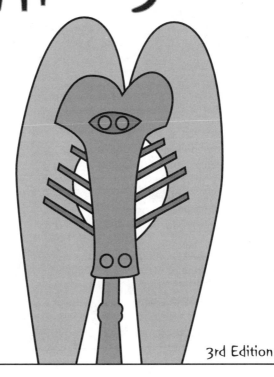

3rd Edition

P.O. Box 578147
Chicago, IL 60657
(773) 276-5911
www.firstbooks.com

3rd edition

Newcomer's Handbook® is a registered trademark of First Books, Inc.

Authors: Mark Wukas and Thor Ringler
Publisher and Editor: Jeremy Solomon
Associate Editor: Bernadette Duperron
Contributors: Amy Bonesteel, Sharon Lanza, Allison Liefer
Maps: Chicago Cartographics
Cover Design: Miles DeCoster
Interior Design/Production: Erin Johnson

CTA transit map is reproduced with the permission of the Chicago Transit Authority.

ISBN 0-912301-39-2

Published by First Books, Inc., P.O. Box 578147, Chicago, IL 60657 773-276-5911.

Printed in Canada

# CONTENTS

# CONTENTS (CONTINUED)

*Apartment hunting, leases and security deposits, renter's insurance, buying a house or condo.*

*Utilities, driver's licenses, parking, voter registration, library cards, newspapers and magazines, online services, broadcast and cable TV, radio, pets, mail delivery, passports, recycling, weather, services for the disabled, gay and lesbian life.*

*Bank accounts, credit cards, income taxes.*

*VCR, computer, television and furniture rentals, haircuts, housecleaning, mail and telephone, storage.*

*Department stores, specialty shops, grocery stores, antique and second-hand shopping, dumpster diving.*

*Types of child care and facilities, public and private schools, colleges and universities.*

*Taking advantage of the city's cultural opportunities.*

WELCOME TO CHICAGO — AND CONGRATULATIONS! YOU ARE now living in the best-kept secret in the United States. What's the secret about Chicago? Simply that it is the most livable big city in America. Newcomers to Chicago from other big cities invariably agree that they enjoy living in Chicago the most. It's easy to see why. No other major metropolis in the country offers its citizens as much access to parks and lakefront, provides such a wide range of world-class cultural and sporting activities, celebrates cultural diversity with annual fests honoring different ethnic groups, and offers shopping comparable to New York and Los Angeles without East or West Coast prices. This book is designed to have you living like a native Chicagoan and enjoying the city in no time.

## CHICAGO'S HISTORY

The area that is now northeastern Illinois was widely populated by Native Americans of the Illinois tribe, hence the name of the state. There is no reliable estimate as to their population, but archaeological excavations downstate have revealed settlements that supported several thousand people.

French voyagers led by Jesuit missionary Fr. Jacques Marquette and explorer Louis Joliet were the first Europeans to pass through Chicago in 1673. Their journey took them down the Mississippi River to Arkansas before they turned back in the face of rumors of hostile natives further south. Marquette and two companions spent the winter of 1674-75 in Chicago in a shelter on the south branch of the Chicago River at what is now Damen Avenue. An easily overlooked cross at the bottom of the Damen bridge marks the site.

Chicago's position near an easily portaged moraine which separated water flowing into the Great Lakes on the east and the Mississippi River on the west made it a widely traveled site. The famed Chicago Portage is marked in a Cook County Forest Preserve near 45th Street and Harlem Avenue. French explorer Robert de la Salle passed by in 1679 on his successful voyage to the mouth of the Mississippi River, and in the following years his men made numerous trips through the region. There was a small French outpost built in the vicinity of Palos Hills, a southwest suburb, but its precise location is uncertain.

**CHICAGO'S FIRST PERMANENT SETTLER WAS JEAN BAPTISTE POINTE DU SABLE, A HAITIAN WHO BUILT A FUR-TRADING POST IN 1779 ON THE LEFT BANK OF WHAT THEN WAS THE MOUTH OF THE CHICAGO RIVER**

European explorers turned to fur trading, making Chicago an even more important crossroads. The region passed into the hands of the British in 1763 after the French and Indian War. Chicago's first permanent settler was Jean Baptiste Pointe du Sable, a Haitian who built a fur-trading post in 1779 on the left bank of what then was the mouth of the Chicago River near the present site of the Equitable Building.

After the American Revolution, Illinois, along with Indiana, Michigan, Ohio and Wisconsin — collectively known as the Northwest Territory — became the territory of the fledgling United States of America. Although the land belonged to the United States, the British stirred up the Indians against the American settlers. In 1812, the garrison and settlers at Fort Dearborn, located on the Chicago River at what now is Michigan Avenue, were ordered to abandon the site for Fort Wayne in Indiana. They didn't make it. The column was attacked along the lake shore at 18th Street and Prairie Avenue and massacred, with only a few survivors saved by natives friendly to the whites. The fort was rebuilt four years later.

Illinois formally joined the Union in 1818. Chicago was incorporated as a town in 1833 and as a city in 1837. Chicago expanded rapidly as settlers poured in from the East, and its importance as a trading center soon made it the most important American city west of the Appalachian Mountains. With the coming of the railroads, Chicago became the hub of the Midwest and the crossroads of the nation.

Chicago grew nonstop until October 1871 when disaster struck. The Great Fire destroyed most of the city as it spread from Mrs. O'Leary's barn — whether her cow was responsible is another issue — on De Koven Street north through downtown and the Near North sides before stopping three days later at Clark Street and Belden Avenue, a block south of Fullerton, and west about as far as Larrabee Street.

Chicago dug in to rebuild. Debris from the fire was pushed into the lake to make landfill for what is today much of Chicago's downtown lakefront. Shanties were quickly built on top of the ashes as citizens vowed to rebuild their lost homes and businesses. One doughty businessman put it best on a sign outside the shack that housed his newly opened real estate office: "All gone but wife, children and energy."

This ambitious fellow wasn't the only person who took advantage of a fantastic opportunity when they saw it. Young East Coast architects came and rebuilt the city in what came to be called the Chicago School, a style never seen before. Daniel Burnham, Louis Sullivan, William Holabird, John Welborn Root, and a young Frank Lloyd Wright were instrumental in rebuilding the city in the decades following the Great Fire.

Chicago proved a popular destination for European immigrants who came in great waves between 1890 and 1910. The Irish, Italians, Poles, Russian Jews, Czechs, Slovakians, Croatians, Serbs — just about every ethnic group imaginable — contributed to the further growth of the city and added to its cacophony of tongues.

After World War I, Prohibition went into effect in 1919, and with it came America's failed experiment with sobriety. It is during the Prohibition era, 1919-1933, that Chicago acquired its reputation as the gangster capital of the world. Most of the mob violence was inspired by turf wars over the lucrative trade in bootleg alcohol, much the same way gangs today battle over drug turf. The 1929 St. Valentine's Day Massacre in a North Clark Street garage stemmed from a war between the North Side Irish gang led by Bugs Moran and the South Side Italian gang led by Al Capone. Fortunately for Moran, he wasn't at the garage that morning, and he retired from bootlegging shortly thereafter. Just for the record, for those who have watched too many "Untouchables" reruns, Chicago is no longer filled with gangsters in fedoras holding tommy guns and standing on running boards. This is not to imply that Chicago is devoid of gangs and gang mayhem — it certainly is not.

ONE DOUGHTY BUSINESSMAN PUT IT BEST ON A SIGN OUTSIDE THE SHACK THAT HOUSED HIS NEWLY OPENED REAL ESTATE OFFICE: "ALL GONE BUT WIFE, CHILDREN AND ENERGY."

## CHICAGO'S GEOGRAPHY

While hills are pretty much non-existent in the city of Chicago (unless you count freeway on-ramps as such), Lake Michigan does offer a striking natural reminder of the days before concrete. Perhaps in no other city are the natural features of the land so overwhelmed by the urban environment of buildings and streets. With the exception of Lake Michigan, it's easy to lose sight of the natural features which originally drew Europeans to the area. First and foremost of these is the Chicago River. From the beginning, the river and its two tributaries (the North Branch and the South Branch) divided the city into three sections: the North Side, the South Side, and the West Side. While the natural barrier of the river has been bridged, literally and frequently, those divisions still exist.

BY DIGGING A CANAL DEEP AND WIDE ENOUGH FOR SHIPPING, AND BY PUTTING LOCKS ON THE CHICAGO RIVER...THE RIVER RAN PERMANENTLY BACKWARDS.

But the most distinguishing characteristic of the Chicago River is its indecisiveness. Long before people arrived on the scene, it could never make up its mind which way it flowed. For much of the year it drained sluggishly into Lake Michigan. In spring and summer, when the lake levels rose, the river would seep west into the Des Plaines River. The end result was stagnant water and wet, marshy ground throughout the region. But there was a hidden payoff to all this: Chicago was the swampy link between the Great Lakes and the Mississippi River basin (of which the Des Plaines River was a part). Business and industry began to arrive, banking on the eventual construction of a canal and railroads.

The uncertain drainage habits of the river were responsible for the city's existence but came back to haunt it later. By the turn of the century, Chicago's population was growing rapidly and the city was producing more sewage and industrial waste than ever; the river was the most convenient place for it. Unfortunately the river emptied into the lake and the drinking water came from the lake. As a result, typhoid was rampant and many people died from it and other water-borne bacterial diseases.

When the Chicago Sanitary & Ship Canal was completed in 1900 the problem was solved. By digging a canal deep and wide enough for shipping and by putting locks on the Chicago River where it emptied into the lake, the river ran permanently backwards. At that time it was the biggest public works project in American history (though the smaller towns downstream were most certainly unimpressed).

One hundred years later, Chicago is still dealing with the indecisive river and its swampy legacy. When it rains hard, basements flood and the river is allowed to flow briefly into the lake to help reduce flooding. Millions of dollars of damage result and city beaches are often closed for days due to bacterial contamination. It may be impossible to imagine the tall grasses and wildlife that once lived here, but the land and the river have not forgotten.

## CHICAGO'S REPUTATION

Before going any further, there are a few popular stereotypes of Chicago that need correcting.

First, although Chicago remains a Daley fiefdom under, Richard M. Daley ("da Mayor"), the eldest son of the late machine strongman Mayor Richard J. Daley, Chicagoans showed that they could control the ballot box with the elections in 1979 of Jane Byrne and of the late Harold Washington in 1983. Corruption is still rampant in Chicago politics, but today it appears to be more of a individual nature and less of an organized condition. And the new Mayor Daley has shown himself to be adept at putting together broad coalitions of ethnic and political groups, something his predecessors in City Hall would have had no interest in even attempting. Nevertheless, Chicago is still one of the most racially segregated metropolitan areas in the United States, and no politician has been able to change that.

DESPITE WHAT THE PEOPLE ON "SATURDAY NIGHT LIVE" THINK, NOT EVERYONE IN CHICAGO REFERS TO THE BEARS AS "DA BEHRZ" AND THE BULLS AS "DA BUHLZ."

Despite what the people on "Saturday Night Live" think, not everyone in Chicago refers to the Bears as "da Behrz" and the Bulls as "da Buhlz." (Actually, Chicagoans say more of a "deh" than a "da.") Native Chicagoans also are notorious for ending sentences with prepositions, as in, "Do you want to come with?" Don't stand there waiting for "me" or "us" to follow "with" — it won't.

There are some things that the newcomer to Chicago needs to learn right away in order not to be recognized as an out-of-towner. First and foremost, it's the "L," not the "subway." "L" is short for elevated, which is Chicago's rapid transit system. Even though some lines do go underground, it's still referred to first as the "L," not the subway.

Next, "the Loop." A portion of Chicago's downtown business and retail district is encircled by "L" tracks, hence the name "the Loop." These tracks surround the Loop on Wabash Avenue on the east, Lake Street on the north, Wells Street on the west and Van Buren Street on the south. State Street, recently renovated to resemble a cozy, turn of the century, gas light shopping district, is home of the venerable Marshall Field's department store as well as "Skate on State," a free outdoor ice-skating rink. Generally speaking, the Loop is any part of the downtown area south of the Chicago River. The area also is referred to as "downtown," but beware: suburbanites often use the term "downtown" to refer to anything in Chicago.

"The Magnificent Mile," the stretch of North Michigan Avenue north of the Chicago River to Oak Street, has replaced the Loop as the city's premier shopping area. It boasts many international retail stores and shopping malls, including Water Tower Place and Chicago Place. It's worth spending a Sunday walking from end to end to get a feel for what North Michigan Avenue has to offer.

CHICAGO, HOME OF THE FIRST SKYSCRAPER, BOASTS THREE OF THE FIVE TALLEST BUILDINGS IN THE WORLD.

Although the Second City comedy troupe still performs at its Old Town location, Chicago itself no longer is the Second City — it's the Third City in population behind New York and Los Angeles. Despite this slip in stature, O'Hare International Airport retains its title as the busiest airport in the world.

Also, Chicago, the home of the first skyscraper, boasts three of the five tallest buildings in the world. The tallest (just beating its recent Malaysian competition in two out of four categories) is the Sears Tower, located outside the southwest corner of the Loop. The fourth tallest is the Standard Oil Building, a white neo-classical building at the north end of Grant Park on Randolph Street. The John Hancock Center, at the north end of Michigan Avenue, is the fifth tallest; it was built in the late 1960s and was the first of Chicago's great towers.

Newcomers complain that everything in Chicago is located on a "corner." When asked for the location of a restaurant or shop, Chicago natives will take the hand-grenade approach and give the nearest corner, e.g., "Webster and Halsted" or "Michigan and Superior," even if the location being sought is in the middle of the block. Keep a sharp eye out for your destination.

# GETTING AROUND IN CHICAGO
*(What no one tells you before you move here.)*

The good news: unlike other large cities in the United States, Chicago offers its residents a variety of transportation options, from car to bus to subway to commuter rail. The bad news: automobile traffic here, and in the suburbs, is horrendous and getting worse.

If you're traveling around the city **by car** keep in mind the following suggestions: budget plenty of time to get where you're going since slow, dense traffic is becoming less of a rush-hour phenomenon and more of a round-the-clock headache; if you can, avoid driving during the morning and late afternoon drive-times when traffic is at its worst; also, be aware that driving in Chicago is not for the faint of heart. Traffic etiquette here is neither generous nor defensive. Drive cautiously because others may not.

The Chicago Transportation Authority's (CTA's) rail transit system, known as **"the L,"** won't win any awards for aesthetic excellence, but it is safe, reliable and fast. The only negative is that unlike, say the New York City subway system, the "L" is not comprehensive. This means, for example, that you cannot take the "L" to Hyde Park (and for many years you couldn't even take it to O'Hare airport!). As would be expected, at rush-hour the "L" is very popular and you may have to squeeze yourself onto a car.

The CTA **bus system** is clean, safe and comprehensive, though at rush-hour buses can feel like sardine tins.

If you are doing a suburb-to-city (or reverse) commute, **Metra**, the suburb-to-city commuter railroad, is the way to go. No kidding; you don't want to be on those highways at rush-hour. Not unless you like breathing traffic fumes.

Chicagoans generally **walk** to their corner store and that's about it. The city is so vast that unless you are in the Loop, walking as a primary means of transportation is not feasible.

Finally, if you're still wondering whether you'll need a car to live in Chicago, the answer is no. An automobile certainly is convenient for grocery shopping, making quick trips, or taking out of town road trips, but trains, buses and taxis are all easily accessible for daily commuting or the trip home after a night out. Regular use of Metra, the CTA's "L" or bus lines and taxis will cost far less than monthly car payments, not to mention astronomical auto insurance rates and the hassle of finding and paying for a parking place.

For more details on getting around Chicago see the "Transportation" chapter.

C HICAGO, LIKE GAUL IN JULIUS CAESAR'S DAY, IS DIVIDED INTO three parts: the North Side, the West Side, and the South Side. Each of these geographical divisions is a mosaic of neighborhoods divided by ethnicity and income that give Chicago its wondrous diversity and vitality. Unlike the eminently forgettable 1975 Paper Lace song "The Night Chicago Died," the city has no official "East Side" (although parts of southeast Chicago on the Indiana border are referred to as the "East Side").

Do not be overwhelmed by Chicago's size. Take it slowly. There's no need to memorize the whole city. Once you find your niche, your neighborhood grocery store, coffee shop, bar, "L" stop, book or record store, you will begin to have a sense of belonging.

A good way to get acquainted with some of Chicago's historical neighborhoods is to take a guided tour. (See the "Cultural Life" chapter of this book for recommendations.)

Like any other big city, Chicago has its share of crime, and no neighborhood is completely safe. However, if you keep your eyes open and use common sense, you should have no problem getting around safely.

There are neighborhoods that it would be best to avoid, and some of them can be deceiving. Uptown, for example, is not a popular neighborhood with newcomers. The high-rises along Sheridan Road may look inviting, but two blocks west is the infamous Kenmore-Winthrop Corridor, a high-crime strip you must enter to reach public transportation. Make no mistake, people do it every day without incident, but there are safer areas for a newcomer to live while getting to know Chicago.

A word about police protection in Chicago. The city is divided into 25 police Districts that serve as neighborhood headquarters for beat and tactical officers. The 25 Districts are grouped into four Areas. If you need police for any emergency, call 911. Officers will be dispatched from the local District and, if necessary, the Area. Otherwise call 312-744-4000 if you have any questions about the location of your nearest District or Area police headquarters.

Chicago has a large immigrant population, and there are old and new neighborhoods where it is possible to imagine you are in a different country. Some of the most notable include: **Argyle**, an Asian (mainly Vietnamese and Chinese) community centered at the intersection of Argyle, Broadway and Sheridan Roads on the North Side; **Koreatown**, a Korean neighborhood west of the Chicago River and east of the Edens Expressway between Foster and Montrose Avenues; **Pilsen**, a Hispanic community west of Halsted Street near 18th Street (see neighborhood profile below); and **West Ridge**, a primarily Indian neighborhood with a mix of Jewish, Assyrian, Pakistani, Thai, Russian, Croatian, Syrian, and Nepalese residents located east of Kedzie and west of Ravenswood along Devon Avenue (see neighborhood profile below). Comprehensive listings and descriptions of these and other areas can be found in *Passport's Guide to Ethnic Chicago* by Richard Lindberg. Also, Chicago Neighborhood Tours (312-742-1190) offers tours through these and other ethnically or historically noteworthy neighborhoods.

The *Newcomer's Handbook* does not attempt to describe every residential neighborhood in Chicago, but it covers many of them. The neighborhoods profiled in this book are all areas which attract large numbers of newcomers to the city. We begin with the downtown neighborhoods, work our way north along the lake, and then come back south for some neighborhoods north and west of the Loop, the South Side and finally eight suburbs. Other pertinent information such as area codes (Chicago's are 312 and 773; the suburbs' are 708, 847, and 630), zip codes, the nearest post office, district police station, local hospital and public library follow each neighborhood description. The nearest rapid-transit stations and the major bus routes through the neighborhood also are listed.

Natives may notice that some neighborhoods have been swallowed by others. The boundaries in this book have been drawn to make learning the city easier for newcomers. Once you get to know Chicago, you can debate and gerrymander neighborhood boundaries at your leisure.

# THE FOLLOWING CHICAGO NEIGHBORHOODS ARE PROFILED:

## NORTH

Cityfront and Streeterville
River North and River West
Gold Coast
Old Town
RANCH Triangle/Clybourn Corridor
Lincoln Park
DePaul/Lincoln Park West
Wrigleyville/Lakeview
North Center
Ravenswood
Lincoln Square
Edgewater
Andersonville
East and West Rogers Park

## WEST

Albany Park
Logan Square
Wicker Park and Bucktown
Ukrainian Village
Taylor Street/University of Illinois-Chicago
Pilsen

## SOUTH

South Loop
The Gap
Bridgeport
Hyde Park
Woodlawn
South Shore
Beverly
Morgan Park

## The following Chicago SUBURBS are profiled:

Evanston
Skokie
Wilmette
Northbrook
Deerfield
Rosemont
Des Plaines
Oak Park

## NORTH

## CITYFRONT AND STREETERVILLE

**Boundaries: North:** Oak Street; **East:** Lake Michigan; **South:** Chicago River; **West:** LaSalle Street

The Cityfront area is located between Michigan Avenue and the lake, north of the Chicago River. It is one of the fastest growing commercial and residential developments in Chicago. Dotted with converted warehouses and new high-rise apartments, the River East neighborhood offers lakefront living at its finest and most expensive.

Navy Pier, a former military training facility, is the docking site of several large ships offering dinner cruises and tours of the Lake Michigan shoreline. More recently it was renovated into a multi-use complex offering great views of downtown Chicago, whether you're walking along the water or rocking the gondola atop one of the world's largest ferris wheels. Though primarily a tourist attraction, Chicagoans come here to see concerts at the Skyline Stage or visit the Chicago Children's Museum.

The new Gateway Park includes a marina, several memorials, including one to Hull House founder Jane Addams, and a theater all within walking distance of River East, Cityfront and Streeterville. There is even a new nine-hole golf course tucked just to the west of Lake Shore Drive.

Streeterville is further north but still east of Michigan Avenue; much of it once was Lake Michigan. The neighborhood was named for Captain George Wellington "Cap" Streeter, one of Chicago's great eccentrics. In 1886, Streeter ran his schooner aground on a sandbar near Michigan Avenue. Unable to dislodge his vessel, Streeter made his home on it. As landfill gradually turned the lake into land, Streeter laid claim to 168 acres of land, basing his claim on an 1821 shoreline survey. After some melees with police and battles in court, Streeter eventually was evicted, but he pressed his claim until his death in 1921.

Streeterville is the heart of North Michigan Avenue, Chicago's blue-chip shopping district, featuring Water Tower Place (Marshall Fields, Lord & Taylor), 900 North Michigan Avenue (Bloomingdale's, Gucci), as well as Neiman Marcus, Saks Fifth Avenue, Crate & Barrel and many more. In addition to other amenities such as restaurants and movie theaters, Streeterville is the home of Northwestern University's Chicago campus, which includes its law and medical schools. Around the corner is the University of Chicago's Graduate School of Business Evening Program. Indeed, you can probably find everything in this neighborhood except a parking place. If you're moving here, and you have a car and intend to keep it, we suggest you rent space in a lot; otherwise you'll be spending all your time trying to find parking.

**Area Code:** 312

**Zip Codes:** 60610, 60611

**Post Offices:** Fort Dearborn, 540 North Dearborn Street, 312-644-7528; Ontario Street Station, 227 East Ontario, 312-642-7698

**Police District:** 18th/East Chicago District (Area 3), 133 West Chicago Avenue, 312-744-8230

**Emergency Hospital:** Northwestern Memorial Hospital, Superior Street and Fairbanks Court, 312-908-2000

**Library:** Harold Washington Library, 400 South State, 312-747-4300

**Transportation - Rapid Transit:** Red (*Howard/Dan Ryan*) Line (stations: Grand, Chicago); Brown (*Ravenswood*) Line (station: Chicago)

**Transportation - Main Bus Routes:** #65 Grand, #66 Chicago, #125 Water Tower Express, #151 Sheridan, #156 LaSalle, #157 Streeterville

## RIVER NORTH AND RIVER WEST

**Boundaries: North:** Chicago Avenue; **East:** LaSalle Street; **South:** Kinzie Street; **West:** Kennedy Expressway

What was once a neighborhood of factories and warehouses has blossomed into Chicago's answer to New York's SoHo, a thriving neighborhood of art galleries. (One local wordsmith dubbed the gallery area "SuHu" since many are on or near Superior and Huron.) Friday afternoon gallery hopping from opening to opening is a favorite pastime for many Chicagoans on their way home from work. In addition to the lively arts scene, River North and River West have more trendy restaurants and dance clubs than you could hope to visit in a month of Friday and Saturday nights. These tourist staples include the Hard Rock Cafe, Planet Hollywood and Harry Caray's, a bar/restaurant founded by the dearly departed Cubs announcer.

The Merchandise Mart, the large building which squats on the north side of the river, has been renovated into a first-class shopping center. Until recently, owned by the Kennedy family for half a century, the Merchandise Mart and the Apparel Center across the street are the center of Chicago's furniture and fashion design industry. Many of the warehouses in the neighborhood have been converted into loft space for offices and apartments. Rents have risen here as they would in any up-and-coming neighborhood, but especially in River North because of its proximity to Michigan Avenue.

River West is a former industrial/manufacturing zone west of the river and east of the Kennedy Expressway. The neighborhood remains a maze of railroad tracks, under- and overpasses, and truncated streets but there are apartments and condos to be found here. And, if you love chocolate, you may just have to live here. The Blommer Chocolate Company, at the corner of Kinzie and Des Plaines Streets, is the kind of factory Charlie (of Willie Wonka fame) lived downwind of. Twenty-four hours a day it lofts a heavenly aroma skyward, making River West one of the best-smelling neighborhoods in the city.

It wasn't always so. A hundred years ago the Chicago River was the largest open sewer in the Midwest and emptied, quite logically, into Lake Michigan, the city's source for drinking water. Nowadays the river actually supports aquatic life of the non-microbial sort. The sight of a turtle paddling along in the shadow of the Merchandise Mart is not the kind of urban scene you might expect this close to the Loop, but River North and River West are full of surprises.

**Area Code:** 312

**Zip Codes:** 60610, 60622

**Post Offices:** Fort Dearborn, 540 North Dearborn Street, 312-644-7603; Merchandise Mart, 222 Merchandise Mart Plaza, 312-321-0386

**Police District:** 18th/East Chicago District (Area 3), 133 West Chicago Avenue, 312-744-8230

**Emergency Hospital:** Northwestern Memorial Hospital, Superior Street and Fairbanks Court, 312-908-2000

**Library:** Harold Washington Library, 400 South State Street, 312-747-4300

**Transportation - Rapid Transit:** Red (*Howard/Dan Ryan*) Line (stations: Grand, Chicago); Brown (*Ravenswood*) Line (stations: Merchandise Mart, Chicago)

**Transportation - Main Bus Routes:** #8 Halsted, #11 Lincoln, #22 Clark, #36 Broadway, #56 Milwaukee, #65 Grand, #66 Chicago, #156 LaSalle

## GOLD COAST

**Boundaries: North:** North Avenue; **East:** Lake Michigan; **South:** Oak Street; **West:** LaSalle Street

The Gold Coast was Chicago's second Millionaires' Row (the first was on the near South Side around 18th Street and Prairie Avenue, where a few old mansions still exist) and remains home to many well-to-do Chicagoans. Although the days when it was the heart of Chicago society have passed, the area retains much of its turn-of-the-century charm. Most of the remaining brownstone and greystone mansions have been converted into condominiums.

Due to the wall of Lake Shore Drive high rises, the Gold Coast sometimes feels like the bottom of a canyon; you might not see the sun until nearly noon. Astor Street has landmark status, protecting it from further development. Despite the walled-in atmosphere, if you use your imagination, you can see the gaslights and hear the carriages and the horses hoofs clopping on the cobblestones.

A landmark along the Clark Street boundary between the Gold Coast and Old Town is Carl Sandburg Village, a combination high-rise and low-rise condominium community constructed in the 1960s on the former site of decrepit, blighted housing. One of the few remaining mansions, and the only one with real grounds, can be found on North Boulevard at the base of Lincoln Park; it is home to the archbishop of Chicago. Unless you have that kind of clout you're not going to find an apartment or condo with a lawn on the Gold Coast. But who needs a lawn when you have Lincoln Park at your doorstep and the lakeshore path and beaches a stone's throw away?

The Gold Coast high rises make for a high population density, but that doesn't keep people from living and living well in the neighborhood. North Michigan Avenue is a brisk walk and Division Street nightlife lies at its feet. Oak Street beach, dramatically situated at the bend in the lake where Michigan Avenue ends, is a favorite lunch spot and a great place to escape from the hustle and bustle of city life. And, speaking of hustle and bustle, unless you want to do an awful lot of it, new residents with cars should consider selling them or finding off-street parking.

**Area Code:** 312

**Zip Codes:** 60610, 60611

**Post Office:** Fort Dearborn, 540 North Dearborn Street, 312-644-7603

**Police District:** 18th/East Chicago District (Area 3), 133 West Chicago Avenue, 312-744-8230

**Emergency Hospital:** Northwestern Memorial Hospital, Superior Street and Fairbanks Court, 312-908-2000

**Libraries:** Harold Washington Library, 400 South State Street, 312-747-4300; Lincoln Park, 1150 West Fullerton Avenue, 312-744-1926

**Transportation - Rapid Transit:** Red (*Howard/Dan Ryan*) Line (station: Clark-Division)

**Transportation - Major Bus Routes:** #11 Lincoln, #22 Clark, #36 Broadway, #65 Grand, #66 Chicago, #70 Division, #72 North, #125 Water Tower Express, #151 Sheridan, #156 LaSalle, #157 Streeterville

## OLD TOWN

**Boundaries: North:** Armitage Avenue; **East:** Clark Street; **South:** North Avenue; **West:** Halsted Street.

Originally a neighborhood made up of German and Irish working-class immigrants, the Old Town Triangle was bounded by North Avenue, Clark Street and Ogden Avenue when it went through to Clark Street (which it no longer does, although you can trace its path if you have a keen eye). The Great Fire of 1871 leveled the area from the lake to Larrabee Street, leaving only the smoldering shell of St. Michael's Church. Undaunted, Old Town residents rebuilt their neighborhood and church quickly; many of the houses in the neighborhood are those built after the fire, although most have since been renovated.

The bohemians from the 1950s and the hippies who hung out on Wells Street in the 1960s have given way to single professionals and young marrieds. Old Town is the closest neighborhood to the Loop and North Michigan Avenue that actually has a neighborhood feel to it (read: houses with front and back lawns larger than high-rise balconies). Make no mistake though: this is an area that has arrived. While attractive and convenient to the best things the city has to offer, housing here is not cheap.

In June, the neighborhood shuts down several streets for the annual Old Town Art Fair. Old Town also is known for being home to the legendary improvisational comedy theater, Second City (1616 North Wells Street), where aspiring John Belushis, Bill Murrays, Chris Farleys and Shelley Longs perform nightly for swarms of city dwellers and tourists alike. A theater district, including the renowned Steppenwolf Theatre, has taken root on Halsted just north of North Avenue. Neighborhood bars are friendly and comfortable. Parking gets tougher closer to the lake.

**Area Codes:** 773 (some 312 near North Avenue)

**Zip Code:** 60614

**Post Office:** Lincoln Park, 2643 North Clark Street, 773-525-5959

**Police District:** 18th/East Chicago District (Area 3), 133 West Chicago Avenue, 312-744-8230

**Emergency Hospitals:** Children's Memorial Medical Center, Lincoln Avenue and Fullerton Avenue, 773-880-4000; Grant Hospital, 550 West Webster Avenue, 773-883-2000

**Library:** Lincoln Park, 1150 West Fullerton Avenue, 312-744-1926

**Transportation - Rapid Transit:** Brown (*Ravenswood*) Line (station: Sedgwick); Red (*Howard/Dan Ryan*) Line (station: North & Clybourn)

**Transportation - Major Bus Routes:** #11 Lincoln, #22 Clark, #36 Broadway, #72 North, #73 Armitage, #151 Sheridan, #156 LaSalle

## RANCH TRIANGLE/CLYBOURN CORRIDOR

**Boundaries: North:** Armitage Avenue; **East:** Halsted Street; **South:** North Avenue: **West:** Clybourn Avenue and Racine Avenue

RANCH stands for the neighborhood boundaries of Racine, Armitage, North, Clybourn and Halsted. The residential area is located east of Clybourn to the western fringes of Old Town (the spire of St. Michael's Church is a few blocks away); here you'll find single-family homes, three-flats and larger apartment buildings. Because it's not as close to the lake as some other near north neighborhoods (about a mile away at this point), the RANCH neighborhood was a relative late bloomer in the North Side gentrification tsunami, going through its upscale makeover in the 1990s.

As recently as the 1980s, Clybourn Avenue was the main artery through an industrial work zone. At night, and on weekends, when the laborers went home and the trucks and freight cars stopped rolling, it was a no-man's land of railroad crossings, hulking factories, and blowing trash. These days just try to find a parking space on Saturday morning; heavy industry has given way to consumer frenzy.

Clybourn now has shopping malls and loft apartments in buildings that once were factories. Some strip malls have also sprung up along Clybourn between North and Webster Avenues. Highlights at the south end of the so-called Clybourn Corridor are a Best Buy electronics store and Sam's Wine and Spirits, which many North Siders consider the best liquor store in the city — it's certainly one of the biggest. There also is a cluster of outlet stores, including a Bed Bath and Beyond, a gourmet supermarket, a Crown Books, and several furniture stores. Further north are the Goose Island Brewery, a micro-brewery and restaurant, and the Webster Place cinemas. In short, you could spend your whole weekend shopping this mile-long stretch.

A few factories remain in the neighborhood, and the community is working to keep them from leaving. If you're tired of shopping but feeling adventurous,you may want to check out the Finkl Steel Company (where Cortland Street crosses the river) for a firsthand glimpse of this neighborhood's industrial heritage. Though there are no official tours, the bay doors on Cortland open into the factory and are frequently left open in the summer to help cool the place down. As you walk or drive by, you may see molten steel being poured.

**Area Code:** 773

**Zip Code:** 60614

**Post Office:** Lincoln Park, 2643 North Clark Street, 773-525-5959

**Police District:** 18th/East Chicago District (Area 3), 133 West Chicago Avenue, 312-744-8230

**Emergency Hospitals:** Children's Memorial Medical Center, Lincoln Avenue and Fullerton Avenue, 773-880-4000; Grant Hospital, 550 West Webster Avenue, 773-883-2000

**Library:** Lincoln Park, 1150 West Fullerton Avenue, 312-744-1926

**Transportation - Rapid Transit:** Red (*Howard/Dan Ryan*) Line (North & Clybourn); Brown (*Ravenswood*) Line (station: Armitage)

**Transportation - Major Bus Routes:** #8 Halsted, #73 Armitage, #72 North

## LINCOLN PARK

**Boundaries: North:** Diversey Parkway; **East:** Lincoln Park; **South:** Armitage Avenue; **West:** Halsted Street

Lincoln Park is the heart of Chicago's North Side. The neighborhood has almost everything you could want (except readily available parking). Housing ranges from high rises to two- and three-flat brownstones to cottages. Unfortunately, there are few, if any, real-estate bargains left in Lincoln Park after more than 30 years of gentrification.

Lincoln Park is lively. You'll find restaurants galore to match any evening's taste and budget; bars and dance clubs run the gamut; and there's little you won't find shopping on Clark Street. The area's most obvious asset is Lincoln Park itself. The rolling 1,200-acre park has extensive playing fields, bike paths, picnic areas and a lovely city zoo with free admission. Beginning in the 1880s, the section from Diversey Parkway north to Ardmore Avenue was constructed primarily on landfill. You may wonder why it's called Diversey Parkway when there's barely a tree on it. It was supposed to be part of Chicago's tree-lined boulevard system (see the Logan Square profile), but the area was swept up in rapid development, and then litigation derailed the project so that today Diversey remains a parkway in name only.

Lincoln Park is steeped in Chicago history. A lone fenced-off mausoleum on LaSalle Drive behind the Historical Society stands as a reminder that the park first served as a city cemetery. Its old name, Lake Park, was changed in 1886 to honor the assassinated president. The grave of the last survivor of the Boston Tea Party is marked by a boulder near Clark Street and Wisconsin Street. The Great Fire of 1871 reached its northernmost extent at roughly Clark and Belden. Two blocks south at 2221 North Clark Street, now a lawn, stood the garage where the infamous St. Valentines Day Massacre took place.

The only drawbacks to this neighborhood — its cost and congestion — are symptoms of its enduring popularity. It remains the preferred address for many Chicagoans.

**Area Code:** 773

**Zip Code:** 60614

**Post Offices:** Lincoln Park, 2643 North Clark Street, 773-525-5959, Lincoln Park Postal Store, 2405 North Sheffield Avenue, 773-929-2742

**Police Districts:** South of Fullerton: 18th/East Chicago District (Area 3), 133 West Chicago Avenue, 312-744-8230; north of Fullerton, Lake Michigan to Clark Street: 23rd/Town Hall District (Area 3), 3600 North Halsted Street, 312-744-8320; north of Fullerton, Clark Street west to the Chicago River: 19th/Belmont District, 2452 West Belmont Avenue (Area 3), 312-744-5983

**Emergency Hospitals:** Children's Memorial Medical Center, Lincoln Avenue and Fullerton Avenue, 773-880-4000; Columbus Hospital, 2520 North Lakeview Avenue, 773-388-7300; Grant Hospital, 550 West Webster Avenue, 773-883-2000

**Libraries:** Lincoln Park, 1150 West Fullerton Avenue, 312-744-1926; John Merlo/Lake View, 644 West Belmont Avenue, 312-744-1139

**Transportation - Rapid Transit:** Red (*Howard/Dan Ryan*) Line (Fullerton); Brown (*Ravenswood*) Line (stations: Armitage, Fullerton, Wellington, Diversey)

**Transportation - Major Bus Routes:** #8 Halsted, #11 Lincoln, #22 Clark, #36 Broadway, #73 Armitage, #74 Fullerton, #76 Diversey, #151 Sheridan, #156 LaSalle

## DEPAUL/LINCOLN PARK WEST

**Boundaries: North:** Diversey Parkway; **East:** Halsted Street; **South:** Diversey Parkway; **West:** Clybourn Avenue

DePaul University is the anchor for this multi-faceted neighborhood just to the west of Lincoln Park proper. Founded in 1898 by the Catholic Vincentian Fathers, DePaul University has expanded over the years to accommodate over 16,000 students. Its Lincoln Park Campus, which lies south of Fullerton Avenue between Halsted Street and Seminary Avenue, is a quiet refuge from the buzz and constant traffic of the surrounding streets.

While the eastern edge of DePaul blends seamlessly into the upscale verve of Lincoln Park, as you move westward the neighborhood changes in character. The area immediately adjacent to the university is younger which makes for a lively nightlife. On weekend nights you'll have a snowball's chance in hell of finding legal parking. Then again, if you live in the neighborhood, you'll have a parking permit and be able to walk to the nightclubs, restaurants, movie theaters and bars along Lincoln Avenue.

West of DePaul, the neighborhood was once firmly working class, home to the blue-collar laborers who worked in the factories along Southport Avenue and the Clybourn Corridor. All that has changed in recent years with the transformation of those old factories into lofts, and major new construction of luxury homes on former abandoned industrial lots. There have also been plenty of tear-downs of older and smaller single family homes to make way for apartment buildings and condos. It's quieter here than further east but by no means dead; there are many excellent restaurants and friendly corner bars, especially along Webster and Wrightwood Avenues.

At its western edge the neighborhood is bounded by Clybourn Avenue and the pace picks up considerably. There's great shopping along Clybourn (see RANCH Triangle/Clybourn Corridor profile in this chapter) and even grimy Ashland (once referred to by the locals as Trashland Avenue) is catching the gentrification bug, with new apartment buildings and former-factory make-overs. Some light industry still exists here giving the area a slight commercial edge. Nevertheless, it seems only a matter of time before the whole neighborhood becomes exclusively residential and service-oriented.

**Area Code:** 773

**Zip Code:** 60614

**Post Offices:** Lincoln Park, 2643 North Clark Street, 773-525-5959; Lincoln Park Postal Store, 2405 North Sheffield Avenue, 773-929-2742

**Police Districts:** South of Fullerton: 18th/East Chicago District (Area 3), 133 West Chicago Avenue, 312-744-8230; North of Fullerton: 19th/Belmont District (Area 3), 2452 West Belmont Avenue, 312-744-5983

**Emergency Hospitals:** Children's Memorial Medical Center, Lincoln

Avenue and Fullerton Avenue, 773-880-4000; Columbus Hospital, 2520 North Lakeview Avenue, 773-388-7300; Grant Hospital, 550 West Webster Avenue, 773-883-2000; Illinois Masonic Medical Center, 836 West Wellington Avenue, 773-975-1600

**Library:** Lincoln Park, 1150 West Fullerton Avenue, 312-744-1926

**Transportation - Rapid Transit:** Red (*Howard/Dan Ryan*) Line (Fullerton); Brown (*Ravenswood*) Line (stations: Armitage, Fullerton, Wellington, Diversey)

**Transportation - Major Bus Routes:** #8 Halsted, #9 Ashland, #11 Lincoln, #73 Armitage, #74 Fullerton, #76 Diversey

# WRIGLEYVILLE/LAKEVIEW

**Boundaries: North:** Irving Park Road; **East:** Lake Shore Drive; **South:** Diversey Parkway; **West:** Ashland Avenue

Wrigleyville, so named for its most famous landmark, Wrigley Field at the corner of Addison and Clark, is the neighborhood of choice for many recent college grads because of its proximity to the lake, its relative affordability and its lively social scene. In fact, Wrigleyville has all of the amenities of Lincoln Park, not to mention its own baseball team, without the prices of its well-to-do neighbor to the south.

Wrigleyville/Lakeview is a dynamic part of town with a large gay population along Broadway between Diversey and Addison. Once the center of Chicago's gay community, the area retains a bohemian air with shops and coffeehouses dotting the retail areas along Broadway and Halsted Street.

Parking can be a problem closer to the lake and when the Cubs play day games. Wrigleyville residents actually look forward to the few Cubs night games because the city tows with a vengeance any car without a neighborhood parking permit (easily obtained at the 44th Ward office on Belmont). Parking has become a cottage industry for some residents, who will rent their garages for up to $10 to fans who don't want to pay $10 to get blocked in the neighborhood parking lots. The large number of sports bars and restaurants means that the area tends to be noisy on nights and weekends throughout the year. Wrigleyville is not the neighborhood for one seeking quiet and solitude.

Although some single family homes exist in Wrigleyville/

Lakeview, most housing is a mixture of new and turn-of-the-century buildings that were designed for apartment living. The recent restoration into deluxe condominiums of several grand buildings near the corner of Surf Street and Broadway has increased the neighborhood's high profile; it may take some effort to find low rental prices here.

For a slightly quieter scene check out the area around Southport Avenue on Lakeview's western edge. Here you can find some single family homes and while Southport has seen an explosion of trendy restaurants and bars in recent years, the pedestrian-friendly Avenue lacks the party-hearty atmosphere of Clark and Halsted. It is also home to one of Chicago's only remaining old-style movie palaces, the Music Box Theater. The fare here is mainly foreign and independent features, and the marvelous interior alone is worth the price of admission. Walking south, past coffeeshops, boutiques, and bowling alleys, you'll spot a landmark of a different sort: the narrow green spire of St. Alphonsus Redemptorist Church. Look up and you may catch a glimpse of the only residents of west Lakeview who actually get a lakeview — the pigeons.

**Area Code:** 773

**Zip Codes:** 60613, 60657

**Post Offices:** Lake View, 1343 West Irving Park Road, 773-327-2932; Graceland Annex, 3635 North Lincoln Avenue, 773-404-5877

**Police Districts:** Lake Michigan to Clark Street: 23rd/Town Hall District (Area 3), 3600 North Halsted Street, 312-744-8320; west of Clark Street to the Chicago River: 19th/Belmont District (Area 3), 2452 West Belmont Avenue, 312-744-5983

**Emergency Hospitals:** St. Joseph Hospital and Health Care Center, 2900 North Lake Shore Drive, 773-665-3000; Illinois Masonic Medical Center, 836 West Wellington Avenue, 773 975-1600; Thorek Hospital & Medical Center, 850 West Irving Park Road, 773-525-6780

**Library:** John Merlo/Lake View, 644 West Belmont Avenue, 312-744-1139

**Transportation - Rapid Transit:** Red (*Howard/Dan Ryan*) Line (stations: Belmont, Addison, Sheridan); Brown (*Ravenswood*) Line (stations: Wellington, Belmont, Southport)

**Transportation - Major Bus Routes:** #8 Halsted, #9 Ashland, #11

Lincoln, #22 Clark, #36 Broadway, #76 Diversey, #77 Belmont, #80
Irving Park, #151 Sheridan, #152 Addison, #156 LaSalle

## NORTH CENTER

**Boundaries: North:** Irving Park Road; **East:** Ashland Avenue; **South:**
Diversey Parkway; **West:** North Branch of Chicago River

Rumor has it that this area got its name from a committee of literal-minded bureaucrats and real estate developers who saw an empty space on a map and a business opportunity. Whatever the real story, the good news is that North Center is nowhere near as dull as its name.

One hundred years ago this was primarily a German neighborhood, but the delis, social clubs, and beer halls with singing waiters have all but faded into collective memory. In the last ten years the eastern edge of North Center, and the Belmont/Lincoln/Ashland intersection in particular, has seen explosive growth. Former department stores, movie palaces, and factories have been tastefully transformed (with original facades intact) into lofts and condos. This gentrification, though slow in coming, was inevitable once the development in North Center's tonier neighbor, Lakeview/Wrigleyville, slowed down. In fact, so strong is the cachet of Lakeview, that you'll hear residents as far west as Damen Avenue claim it as their neighborhood. Go figure.

It's true that North Center is not as trendy (yet), popular, or pleasant to pronounce as its easterly neighbor, but it is considerably quieter, and you can even park your car on the street at night. The Ravenswood "L" (Brown Line) runs along the eastern edge of the neighborhood and is the commute of choice for those who work downtown. **Roscoe Village**, a mini-neighborhood centered around Roscoe Street between Damen and Western Avenues, is a charming low-key area with restaurants, antique shops, and older stores. Lincoln Avenue, North Center's main shopping drag, offers a mishmash of old-world and new-age businesses where chic blends into kitsch and comes out . . . unique. And, last but not least, for the real Chicago experience — driving way too fast, radio blaring, windows open, straight as an arrow down a pot-holed, neon-drenched street lined with used-car lots, bowling alleys, strip malls, and fast food joints — check out Western Avenue, one of the longest, continuous city streets in the country.

Once you come to your senses, get out of your car and take a walk.

You'll find plenty of restaurants, picture-perfect neighborhood bars, and quiet tree-lined streets with lovely homes scattered throughout North Center.

> **Area Code:** 773
>
> **Zip Codes:** 60613, 60618, 60657
>
> **Post Offices:** Graceland (Postal Finance Station), 3024 North Ashland Avenue, 773-248-8494; Graceland Annex, 3635 North Lincoln Avenue, 773-404-5877; Lakeview, 1343 West Irving Park Road, 773-327-2932
>
> **Police District:** 19th/Belmont District (Area 3), 2542 West Belmont Avenue, 312-744-5983
>
> **Emergency Hospitals:** Illinois Masonic Medical Center, 836 West Wellington Avenue, 773-975-1600; Ravenswood Hospital/Medical Center, 4550 North Winchester Avenue, 773-878-4300
>
> **Libraries:** Hamlin Park, 2205 West Belmont Avenue, 312-744-0166; Sulzer, 4455 North Lincoln Avenue, 312-744-7616
>
> **Transportation - Rapid Transit:** Brown (*Ravenswood*) Line (stations: Paulina, Addison, Irving Park)
>
> **Transportation - Major Bus Routes:** #9 Ashland, #11 Lincoln, #49 Western, #50 Damen, #76 Diversey, #77 Belmont, #80 Irving Park, #152 Addison

## RAVENSWOOD

**Boundaries: North:** Foster Avenue; **East:** Clark Street; **South:** Irving Park Road; **West:** Damen Avenue

The Ravenswood neighborhood was named for Ravenswood Avenue, which runs alongside the Chicago and North Western Railway. The neighborhood grew in popularity in the 1860s when the C&NW opened a station at Wilson Avenue and then burgeoned during the 1880s and 1890s when streetcar lines reached the area. Ravenswood is a family neighborhood filled with wonderful vintage buildings and multi-unit apartment complexes; it's an area where renovation and rehabilitation have taken precedence over raze and ruin. There has been some movement to nominate part of the neighborhood, the East Ravenswood Historic District, to the National Register of Historic Places.

Right across the street from the neighborhood's southwest corner is one of Chicago's best known funerary landmarks, Graceland Cemetery. Here you can marvel (or wince) at the sumptuous sepulchers of former captains of industry: Pullman, Potter, Getty, and the list goes on. It's also a great place to go for a walk, if you like solitude, trees, and quiet. Ravenswood is quiet too, but considerably more lively. While the neighborhood lacks the restaurants and nightlife of its neighbors, Wrigleyville and Andersonville, it's conveniently close to them.

The easy commuting distance to both downtown and the North Shore suburbs (thanks to the Metra/Union Pacific North Line) and a large number of churches make Ravenswood feel like a small suburb within the city. Community organizations abound, and a yearly garden walk is only one of the activities residents organize. "There's a real sense of community here," said one long-time resident. "You know your neighbors and look out for one another."

**Area Code:** 773

**Zip Codes:** 60613, 60640

**Post Offices:** Ravenswood, 2522 West Lawrence Avenue, 773-561-9294; Lakeview, 1343 West Irving Park Road, 773-327-2932; Uptown, 4850 North Broadway, 773-561-8916

**Police District:** 19th/Belmont District (Area 3), 2452 West Belmont Avenue, 312-744-5983

**Emergency Hospitals:** Methodist Hospital, 5025 North Paulina Street, 773-271-9040; Ravenswood Hospital Medical Center, 4550 North Winchester Avenue, 773-878-4300

**Library:** Sulzer, 4455 North Lincoln Avenue, 312-744-7616

**Transportation - Rapid Transit:** Brown (*Ravenswood*) Line (stations: Irving Park, Montrose, Damen, Western); Metra/Union Pacific North Line (station: Ravenswood)

**Transportation - Major Bus Routes:** #11 Lincoln, #22 Clark, #50 Damen, #78 Montrose, #80 Irving Park, #81 Lawrence, #92 Foster

## LINCOLN SQUARE

**Boundaries: North:** Foster Avenue; **East:** Damen Avenue; **South:** Irving Park Road; **West:** Chicago River

Lincoln Square, the area where Lincoln Avenue snakes into the intersection of Western and Lawrence Avenues, is an old German neighborhood that grew during the late 19th century. Plenty of German shops, restaurants and bars remain, as well as Germans themselves; it's not unusual to hear long-time residents chatting *auf Deutsch*. Meier's Deli, on Lincoln Avenue, is definitely worth a visit. You will find excellent homemade German cheese, sausages and chocolate. Today, however, the neighborhood is not homogeneous by any means. Amidst the cafes in the strip between Lincoln and Lawrence there is a row of Greek restaurants that give the area a distinctly Mediterranean flavor as well as several nearby Korean, Mexican and Baltic establishments which reflect this neighborhood's truly international make-up.

Pluses include one of the largest public libraries in the city and Chicago Park District facilities for children and adults. The Lincoln Square Mall, on Lincoln between Lawrence and Leland Avenues, offers everything from homemade German sausages to fresh produce at an open-air farmer's market on Tuesday mornings during the summer months. Look for the Sears department store, which will have anything and everything you might need for your home. Housing in the Lincoln Square neighborhood is a typical mix of architecturally uninspired single family homes, apartments and a small but growing number of condominiums with vintage touches. Between Western Avenue and the Chicago River you can find a pocket of lovely classic Chicago bungalows surrounded by more affordable multi-unit apartment buildings.

For the architecturally inclined Lincoln Square contains a rare treat. Louis Sullivan's last work (1921), the Krause Music Store, can be found at 4611 North Lincoln Avenue. Directly across the street is the flickering marquee of the bargain basement Davis Theater, which shows second-run Hollywood movies and occasional independent films. South of the Davis are the new digs of the popular and long-lived Old Towne School of Folk Music. The contrast is typical for Lincoln Avenue. From swanky cafes to greasy spoons, and Euro-chic to retro-thrift; faux-old-world charm to generic Americana, the street offers something for everyone. The same goes for the Lincoln Square neighborhood itself.

**Area Code:** 773

**Zip Codes:** 60618, 60625

**Post Office:** Ravenswood, 2522 West Lawrence Avenue, 773-561-9294

**Police District:** 19th/Belmont District (Area 3), 2452 West Belmont Avenue, 312-744-5983

**Emergency Hospitals:** Methodist Hospital, 5025 North Paulina Street, 773-271-9040; Ravenswood Hospital Medical Center, 4550 North Winchester Avenue, 773-878-4300; Swedish Covenant Hospital, 5145 North California Avenue, 773-878-8200

**Library:** Sulzer Regional, 4455 North Lincoln Avenue, 312-744-7616

**Transportation - Rapid Transit:** Brown (*Ravenswood*) Line (stations: Irving Park, Montrose, Damen,Western)

**Transportation - Major Bus Routes:** #11 Lincoln, #49 Western, #50 Damen, #78 Montrose, #80 Irving Park, #81 Lawrence, #92 Foster

## EDGEWATER

**Boundaries: North:** Devon Avenue; **East:** Lake Michigan; **South:** Foster Avenue; **West:** Ravenswood Avenue

Edgewater meant elegance in the era between World Wars I and II when the Edgewater Beach Hotel was the North Shore spot for fine dining and dancing. Alas, no longer. The Edgewater Hotel was torn down in the 1970s to make way for a high-rise apartment complex, as were most of the other fine old lakeshore mansions that surrounded it. One survivor is the flamingo pink building which houses the Edgewater Beach Apartments. The high rise boom of the 1960s and 1970s is over, and if you go inland a few blocks (skipping the blighted Kenmore-Winthrop Corridor), you'll find that parts of Edgewater include big, friendly houses that are being rehabbed by a new, often young, generation of home-owners. At its northern edge, Edgewater is home to Loyola University and many students live in the surrounding area. The neighborhood is also home to large numbers of Hispanic and Asian families as well as retirees, many of whom live in the high rises lining the lake. With its convenient location; easy access to Lakeshore Drive, the Howard/Red "L" line, and the Clark Street bus, and with the popular Andersonville located in the southern end of Edgewater, as well as the recent Clark Street and Senn Park renovation and the neighborhood's very active community council, the E.C.C., this area will likely become the next great neighborhood in north Chicago. While real estate prices here are still a bargain, they're on their way up.

Lincoln Park and the lakefront path both come to an end at Edgewater's southeast corner. The beaches (Hollywood-Ardmore and Foster Avenue) are beautiful and offer excellent views of the shoreline to the north. On clear days you can make out the lakeshore campus of Northwestern University in Evanston. Looking eastward, out across the lake, you will spot a squat, cylindrical shape that hovers about two miles off the shoreline. Don't be misled by locals who may try to convince you that it is (1) a giant floating storage tank for industrial waste, (2) a casino, or (3) the new Bears stadium. It's actually a water intake crib, one of three (if you look south you can see the others) that provides the city with its fresh water.

**Area Code:** 773

**Zip Codes:** 60640, 60660

**Post Offices:** Rogers Park, 1723 West Devon Avenue, 773-508-1200; Uptown, 4850 North Broadway, 773-561-8916

**Police Districts:** South of Peterson Avenue: 20th/Foster Avenue District (Area 3), 1940 West Foster Avenue, 312-744-8330; north of Peterson Avenue: 24th/Rogers Park District (Area 3), 6464 North Clark Street, 312-744-5907

**Emergency Hospitals:** Edgewater Medical Center, 5700 North Ashland Avenue, 773-878-6000; Ravenswood Hospital Medical Center, 4550 North Winchester Avenue, 773-878-4300; Weiss Memorial Hospital, 4646 North Marine Drive, 773-878-8700

**Library:** Edgewater, 1210 West Elmdale Avenue, 312-744-0718

**Transportation - Rapid Transit:** Red (*Howard/Dan Ryan*) Line (stations: Berwyn, Bryn Mawr, Thorndale, Granville)

**Transportation - Major Bus Routes:** #22 Clark, #36 Broadway, #50 Damen, #84 Peterson, #92 Foster, #136 Sheridan/LaSalle Express, #147 Outer Drive Express, #151 Sheridan, #155 Devon

## ANDERSONVILLE

**Boundaries: North:** Bryn Mawr; East: Glenwood Avenue; **South:** Foster Avenue; **West:** Ravenswood Avenue

Who needs Wisconsin or Minnesota? If you're looking for Scandinavian history and heritage, you can find it here. Andersonville, located in a half square mile in the southwest corner of Edgewater, is an old Swedish neighborhood first settled in the mid-19th century. Although most of the Swedes are long gone, Andersonville retains some of its ethnic flavor in its architecture and neighborhood bakeries, gift shops and the Swedish American Museum at 5211 North Clark Street (773-728-8111). The neighborhood has evolved into an ethnic mosaic easily seen by the restaurants ranging from the old Swedish to Persian to Asian to Mexican and beyond.

Housing in this neighborhood consists primarily of attractive, large single family homes and stylish three-flats. While less expensive than the more well-known areas to the south, Andersonville is no longer the delightful bargain it once was. Word is out. For those without a car, there is one drawback to this neighborhood: no easy access to the "L."

Andersonville is a bit of a mecca for women business owners, many of whom own shops, restaurants and book stores on Clark Street (Women & Children First, a feminist bookstore, is known for its book selection and author signings). Also the Kopi Travelers Cafe is one of the city's more notable poetry salon/coffeehouses and neo-beatniks are attracted to its caffeinated confines. A large gay and lesbian population thrives in Andersonville, and many businesses, such as video rental stores, bookstores and restaurants are owned by and cater to this crowd.

Two of the city's best bakeries are located here. For freshly-baked pita bread and scrumptious spinach pies, check out the Middle Eastern Bakery on Foster Avenue between Clark and Ashland. Finally, for your own sake, do *not* buy a coffeecake from the Swedish Bakery at 5348 North Clark Street. You will devour the whole thing and wind up guilt-ridden, covered with crumbs, and completely satisfied. On second thought . . .

**Area Code:** 773

**Zip Code:** 60640

**Post Office:** Uptown, 4850 North Broadway, 773-561-8916

**Police District:** 20th/Foster Avenue District (Area 3), 1940 West Foster Avenue, 312-744-8330

**Emergency Hospitals:** Edgewater Medical Center, 5700 North Ashland Avenue, 773-878-6000; Methodist Hospital, 5025 North Paulina Street, 773-271-9040; Ravenswood Hospital Medical Center, 4550 North Winchester Avenue, 773-878-4300; Weiss Memorial Hospital, 4646 North Marine Drive, 773-878-8700

**Library:** Edgewater, 1210 West Elmdale Avenue, 312-744-0718

**Transportation - Rapid Transit:** Red (*Howard/Dan Ryan*) Line (station: Berwyn)

**Transportation - Major Bus Routes:** #22 Clark, #50 Damen, #92 Foster

## EAST AND WEST ROGERS PARK

**Boundaries: North:** Evanston; **East:** Lake Michigan; **South:** Devon Avenue; **West:** Chicago River

Originally Rogers Park was a village along the old post road (Clark Street) to Green Bay, Wisconsin, and a suburb of Evanston located ten miles north of the Loop. As Chicago grew Rogers Park was annexed by the city in 1893. Once perceived as a predominantly Jewish neighborhood, Rogers Park today is a confluence of every conceivable ethnic group with a large number of Hispanic families (recent arrivals, coincidentally, are Russian Jews).

Rogers Park is a unique neighborhood that has a quasi-1960s flavor to it, thanks to the many social activists, artists and ex-hippies living here. The Heartland Cafe, which publishes its own liberal newspaper espousing community issues, is also located in Rogers Park. Because it's situated between Loyola University and Northwestern University in Evanston, Rogers Park has a large student population, and this means the neighborhood's counter-cultural legacy is in some way continually being reborn. In addition, the neighborhood has a lively arts community.

East Rogers Park, a neighborhood filled with low-rise apartment buildings and two- and three-flat houses, offers truly affordable living close to Lake Michigan. Be aware, though, that gang activity and crime are a definite concern in this neighborhood. As a rule of thumb, the streets with more single family and two- and three-flat homes tend to be safer than streets with a predominance of apartment buildings. West Rogers Park, i.e., west of Ridge Avenue, has fewer apartment buildings and more single family homes. Late spring is probably the best time to find an apartment here, keeping in mind the seasonally fluctuating student population. In the summer, residents have little reason to leave their neighborhood on weekends: Loyola Park and eight beaches extend south from Evanston like pearls on a string.

West Rogers Park (also known as **West Ridge**) is a haven for newly arrived immigrants, and Devon Avenue, which runs along its southern edge, is the main shopping strip. Here are stores selling every conceivable foodstuff — Indian, Syrian, Pakistani, Kosher — and restaurants to please every palate. On weekend nights the sidewalks are teeming, a shoulder to shoulder mass of humanity. It's a slow-motion version of the Loop in rush hour, with saris and slippers standing in for suits and wing tips. If you're looking for a truly diverse neighborhood or just looking for a great, inexpensive meal, West Rogers Park is the place to go.

**Area Code:** 773

**Zip Codes:** 60626, 60645

**Post Office:** Rogers Park, 1723 West Devon Avenue, 773-508-1200

**Police District:** 24th/Rogers Park District (Area 3), 6464 North Clark Street, 312-744-5907

**Emergency Hospitals:** Edgewater Medical Center, 5700 North Ashland Avenue, 773-878-6000; St. Francis Hospital of Evanston, 355 Ridge Avenue, Evanston, 847-316-4000

**Library:** Rogers Park, 6709 North Clark Street, 312-744-0156

**Transportation - Rapid Transit:** Red (*Howard/Dan Ryan*) Line (stations: Loyola, Morse, Jarvis, Howard); Metra/Union Pacific North Line (station: Rogers Park)

**Transportation - Major Bus Routes:** #22 Clark, #49B North Western, #50 Damen, #93 N. California, #96 Lunt, #147 Outer Drive Express, #151 Sheridan, #155 Devon

## WEST

## ALBANY PARK

**Boundaries: North:** Foster Avenue; **East:** North Branch of Chicago River; **South:** Montrose Avenue; **West:** Pulaski Road

While intellectuals debate the definition and implementation of multiculturalism, Albany Park is living proof that it exists, and that it works. With a foreign born population of 50 percent, it's easy to walk down the streets here on a hot summer night and convince yourself that you're in another country. But which one? When it comes to food, the questions can get overwhelming, especially on an empty stomach. Kimchee? Falafel? Fajita? Pad Thai? Happily, the answers are all equally delicious.

Albany Park is best known for the concentration of Korean restaurants and grocery stores along Lawrence Avenue, known as **Koreatown**. In fact the mile-long section of Lawrence between the river and Pulaski Road has been given the honorary name of Seoul Drive. The neighborhood here is always busy, especially on the weekends, and traffic frequently slows to a crawl. But don't let the hustle and bustle of the avenues mislead you; there are plenty of practical and quiet reasons why people choose to live here.

Public transportation for one. The northern end of the Ravenswood "L" (Brown Line) comes to earth in Albany Park after crossing the Chicago River. The resulting street-level crossings, with flashing red lights, warning bells, and barriers, give the southeast corner of the neighborhood the feel of a small town. This area is also bounded, and very much defined, by the river; along it you will find quiet streets, abundant greenery, and plenty of attractive single family-homes and apartments.

Moving westward, the neighborhood recovers its big city edge but remains quiet and residential: easy access to the Kennedy and Edens expressways are also perks. It should be noted that Albany Park is poorer than neighboring Lincoln Square and parts of it are rough. In particular, newcomers unused to the harder edges of urban life may want to think twice before moving into the area north of Lawrence and east of Kedzie.

Albany Park's current ethnic diversity is not surprising. It has always been known as a stepping-stone neighborhood, a place where generations of immigrants have cut their teeth on the New World before moving on to the suburbs. What is surprising is that the natives haven't discovered it.

**Area Code:** 773

**Zip Code:** 60625

**Post Offices:** Kedzie-Grace, 3750 North Kedzie Avenue, 773-478-6714; Ravenswood, 2522 West Lawrence Avenue, 773-561-9294

**Police District:** 17th /Albany Park District (Area 5), 4461 North Pulaski Road, 312-744-8346

**Emergency Hospitals:** Methodist Hospital, 5025 North Paulina Street, 773-271-9040; Ravenswood Hospital, 4550 North Winchester Avenue, 773-878-4300; Swedish Covenant Hospital, 5145 North California Avenue, 773-878-8200

**Libraries:** Independence, 3548 West Irving Park Road, 312-744-0900; Mayfair, 4400 West Lawrence Avenue, 312-744-1254

**Transportation - Rapid Transit:** Brown (*Ravenswood*) Line (stations: Francisco, Kedzie, Kimball)

**Transportation - Major Bus Routes:** #53 Pulaski, #78 Montrose, #81 Lawrence, #82 Kimball/Homan, #93 North California

## LOGAN SQUARE

**Boundaries: North:** Diversey Avenue; **East:** Western Avenue; **South:** Armitage Avenue; **West:** Kimball Avenue

Before the BMWs and Land Rovers were there to turn our heads and alert us to the social standing of their occupants, horses and carriages served the same function. What better place to show off your horsepower (albeit in the single digits) than a tree-lined boulevard on the outskirts of the city? Originally a European idea, Chicago began its own system of boulevards in the mid-nineteenth century. Completed in the 1870s, the boulevards stretched inland from the lake at Lincoln Park through seven parks and finally met up with the lake again at Jackson Park. Together they form an uninterrupted twenty mile belt of greenery with Logan Square (and its namesake neighborhood) at its northwest corner.

Nowadays you won't see many horse-drawn carriages in Logan Square (or many BMWs for that matter) but the boulevards are still there, as are the greystones and apartment buildings that front them. Gentrification has been slow to come here and, unlike booming

Bucktown to the east, Logan Square is still predominantly poor and working class. But you'd never guess that from its housing stock: the architectural styles (which range from Art Nouveau and Prairie to Renaissance Revival and Gothic) show a variety which few neighborhoods can match.

You won't find many coffeeshops or trendy boutiques here, but Logan Square has lower rents than its easterly neighbors and is conveniently located for commuters; the Kennedy Expressway cuts through its northeastern corner and the O'Hare/Congress/Douglas Blue Line runs parallel to Milwaukee Avenue. At street level there are excellent thrift stores, fruit markets, and Mexican restaurants along Milwaukee Avenue, and the Logan Theater shows second-run Hollywood films for a song ($2 at press time). For a real time-warp, don't miss the local landmark: Margie's Candies (at the southwest corner of Western and Armitage Avenues). An honest to goodness ice cream parlor, Margie's has been dishing out homemade ice cream and fudge sauce for over seventy-five years. A word of caution: newcomers considering Logan Square should carefully check out this neighborhood before moving in. Logan Square has an edge that other neighborhoods to the east do not and gang activity, though diminishing, is for real here.

**Area Code:** 773

**Zip Code:** 60647

**Post Office:** Logan Square, 2339 North California Avenue, 773-484-1474

**Police District:** 14th/Shakespeare District (Area 5), 2150 North California Avenue, 312-744-8290

**Emergency Hospitals:** St. Elizabeth's Hospital, 1431 North Claremont Avenue, 773-278-2000; Norwegian American Hospital, 1044 North Francisco Avenue, 773-292-8200

**Library:** Logan Square, 3255 West Altgeld Street, 312-744-5295

**Transportation - Rapid Transit:** Blue (*O'Hare/Congress/Douglas*) Line (stations: Western, California, Logan Square)

**Transportation - Major Bus Routes:** #49 Western, #52 Kedzie/California, #56 Milwaukee, #73 Armitage, #74 Fullerton, #76 Diversey, #82 Kimball/Homan

## WICKER PARK AND BUCKTOWN

**Boundaries: North:** Fullerton Avenue; **East:** Kennedy Expressway;
**South:** Division Street; **West:** Western Avenue

Blessed with gorgeous and once forgotten Victorian, Queen Anne and Italianate mansions, in the late 1980s and 1990s Wicker Park became a slacker haven and music hub (rock artists including Liz Phair, Veruca Salt and Urge Overkill all called it home at one time). Today the "the hippest neighborhood in Chicago," as proclaimed by several magazines, is in a state of flux. Rapid gentrification and the opening of new clubs and restaurants are causing many residents who came to the area for its bohemian atmosphere, inexpensive rent and racial mix to feel that their neighborhood may soon become indistinguishable from Lincoln Park. Their fears are not groundless. Rents have risen with property values, making bargains much harder to come by.

Historically, Wicker Park and Bucktown were bastions of European immigration, with Germans holding sway in Wicker Park and Poles in Bucktown. Wicker Park is named for the small park in the middle of the neighborhood; Bucktown got its name because the poorer immigrants kept goats in their backyards. The boundary between the neighborhoods is the elevated (not the "L" tracks) Soo line railroad track. When traveling in a car, the shadow from that overpass is the only indication that you've crossed over; beyond that it's difficult to distinguish one neighborhood from the other. Both Wicker Park and Bucktown fell on hard times during the flight to the suburbs after World War II, but they retain some of their original flavor. Latinos filled the post-war void and remain the area's largest ethnic group — although that's changing fast as gentrification creeps north and west.

Because of the formerly low rents, there are still a large number of artists in both neighborhoods. "Around the Coyote" is an annual arts festival that draws increasingly large numbers to the area for a weekend each fall (much to the chagrin of neighborhood old-timers).

In recent years Wicker Park/Bucktown has become a favorite destination for savvy diners, and the intersection of Damen, Milwaukee, and North Avenues a kind of gastronomical hub. Nearby there are scores of restaurants, and hungry crowds of city-dwellers and suburbanites roam the streets. Many of the restaurants are French (or high-concept variants thereof — the higher the concept, the higher the price) but you will also find Mexican, Asian, Chilean, and Italian. Valet and permit parking have also arrived and vehicular mayhem reigns, especially on the weekends. For the brave and ravenous, the choice is clear.

For the merely hungry, the majorly hungover, or the still-waiting-on-that-freelance-paycheck crowd there's the Busy Bee restaurant/diner, just south of the Damen "L" stop. They've been serving breakfast, lunch, and Polish specialties here for over thirty years and the city is appreciative; beaming headshots of local politicians and celebrities line the walls and the place is always packed.

**Area Codes:** 312 and 773

**Zip Codes:** 60614, 60622, 60647

**Post Offices:** Wicker Park, 1635 West Division Street, 773-278-1919; Logan Square, 2339 North California Avenue, 773-489-1474

**Police District:** 14th/Shakespeare District (Area 5), 2150 North California Avenue, 312-744-8290

**Emergency Hospitals:** St. Elizabeth's Hospital, 1431 North Claremont Avenue, 773-278-2000; St. Mary of Nazareth Hospital Center, 2233 West Division Street, 312-770-2000

**Libraries:** Damen Avenue, 2056 North Damen Avenue, 312-744-6022; Eckhart Park, 1371 West Chicago Avenue, 312-746-6069; West Town, 1271 North Milwaukee Avenue, 312-744-1473

**Transportation - Rapid Transit:** Blue (*O'Hare/Congress/Douglas*) Line (stations: Division, Damen, Western, California)

**Transportation - Major Bus Routes:** #9 Ashland, #49 Western, #50 Damen, #56 Milwaukee, #70 Division, #72 North, #73 Armitage, #74 Fullerton

## UKRAINIAN VILLAGE

**Boundaries: North:** Division Street; **East:** Ashland Avenue; **South:** Superior Street; **West:** Western Avenue

The name says it all: the neighborhood was settled by Ukrainian immigrants who came to Chicago at the turn of the century. Unlike other ethnic enclaves in Chicago, the Ukrainian stamp remains on the neighborhood with its onion-domed churches and signs in the Cyrillic alphabet. The Holy Trinity Orthodox Cathedral designed by famed Chicago architect Louis Sullivan is well worth a visit as is the Ukrainian National Museum.

The rapidly-growing eastern section of the neighborhood (from Damen to Ashland) has attracted large numbers of Hispanic families as well as artists and students seeking bargains. There are, however, still descendants of the Eastern Europeans who founded the area; many times, newcomers find themselves living side-by-side with the children and grandchildren of the original inhabitants.

Architecturally, the neighborhood has everything from mansions on Hoyne to two- and three-flat greystones to workers' cottages, which have brought a good number of rehabbers and do-it-yourselfers to the area. Many buildings still have the original ornate designs and finely crafted details that were long ago removed from buildings in other neighborhoods.

**Area Code:** 312

**Zip Codes:** 60612, 60622

**Post Offices:** Wicker Park, 1635 West Division Street, 773-278-1919; Midwest, 2419 West Monroe, 312-243-1603

**Police District:** 13th/Wood District (Area 4), 937 North Wood Street, 312-746-8350

**Emergency Hospitals:** St. Elizabeth's Hospital, 1431 North Claremont Avenue, 773-278-2000; St. Mary of Nazareth Hospital Center, 2233 West Division Street, 312-770-2000; Rush-Presbyterian St. Luke's Medical Center, 1653 West Congress Parkway, 312-942-5000

**Libraries:** Eckhart Park, 1371 West Chicago Avenue, 312-746-6069; West Town, 1271 North Milwaukee Avenue, 312-744-1473

**Transportation - Rapid Transit:** None

**Transportation - Major Bus Routes:** #9 Ashland, #49 Western, #50 Damen, #65 Grand, #66 Chicago, #70 Division

# TAYLOR STREET/UNIVERSITY OF ILLINOIS-CHICAGO

**Boundaries: North:** Harrison Street; **East:** Halsted Street; **South:** Roosevelt Road; **West:** Ashland Avenue

At the turn of the century, the Taylor Street neighborhood, also known as Little Italy, was an immigrant ghetto in which the famed progressive social worker Jane Addams and the Hull House served the community for many years. Although the Hull House complex has been razed, one building remains as a museum and cultural center.

Taylor Street was a thriving, solidly Italian neighborhood until Mayor Daley *père* decided in the early 1960s he needed a place to build the Chicago campus of the University of Illinois (UIC). The university originally was planned for what is now Dearborn Park, but Daley was unable to make a deal at the time with the railroads that owned the land. As the university continues to grow (what once was a commuter college now has dormitories), the neighborhood loses a little more of its ethnic color. The strip of Italian restaurants on Taylor Street and Vernon Park Place are a fine example of what the entire area once looked like. There is some building renovation taking place in the Taylor Street neighborhood, but most of the construction consists of new townhomes to accommodate the medical personnel who want to live close to the cluster of large hospitals in the area.

UIC is planning a large southward expansion of its campus in the next five years, which is good news for construction companies and students. But neighbors to the south are wary. Given the college's track record of swallowing up low-income neighborhoods, they have good reason.

**Area Code:** 312

**Zip Code:** 60607

**Post Office:** Main Post Office, 433 West Harrison Street, 312-765-3225

**Police District:** 12th/Monroe District (Area 4), 100 South Racine Avenue, 312-746-8396

**Emergency Hospitals:** Cook County Hospital, 1835 West Harrison Street, 633-6000; Rush-Presbyterian St. Luke's Hospital, 1653 West Congress Parkway, 942-5000; University of Illinois Hospital and Clinics, 1740 West Taylor Street, 996-9634

**Library:** Roosevelt, 1055 West Roosevelt Road, 312-746-9200

**Transportation - Rapid Transit:** Blue (*O'Hare/Congress/Douglas*) Line (stations: U of I/Halsted, Racine, Polk, Medical Center)

**Transportation - Major Bus Routes:** #8 Halsted, #9 Ashland, #12 Roosevelt, #37 Sedgwick/Ogden, #60 Blue Island

## PILSEN

**Boundaries: North:** 16th Street; **East:** Canal Street; **South:** South Branch of Chicago River; **West:** Damen Avenue

In recent decades, it's been a familiar story: a poor neighborhood with attractive but run-down housing stock is "discovered" by artists, gradually rehabbed, and ultimately overrun with yuppies and new development. What with rent and property tax hikes, the original inhabitants move on to other, as-yet-undiscovered, neighborhoods. For better or for worse, Pilsen is the latest of these discoveries. Given its proximity to the Loop, public transit, and three different expressways, this was probably inevitable. Scarce comfort to the thousands of Hispanic families who currently live here.

Pilsen, also known as the Lower West Side, was originally settled by Czechs, Poles and Bohemians (the neighborhood was named after a city in Bohemia) and later became home to more recent immigrants from Lithuania, Germany, and Italy. For many years it was an industrial neighborhood whose inhabitants worked in the factories, lumberyards, and docks along the Chicago River and the Sanitary & Ship Canal. Beginning in the 1950s, Mexicans and Puerto-Ricans began moving into the area, and today it has the highest percentage of Hispanic residents (88 percent) of any Chicago neighborhood.

Most new development in Pilsen is happening in the area east of Morgan Street. The activity is centered on Halsted Street, a one-time commercial district whose stores and factories have become artists' studios. Rents here are cheap (but quickly rising) however you'll have to travel west for groceries or shopping. Of course, if you're living on cigarettes and oil paint fumes, that shouldn't be a problem.

Eighteenth Street, the main East-West artery through the neighborhood, is hopping at all hours. There are restaurants aplenty, bars galore, and neighborhood groceries up the yinyang. Definitely check out the Fiesta del Sol which takes place the first weekend in August and offers live music, games, rides and food. Many of the buildings in Pilsen are old and funky but there's no shortage of apartments. Just don't stray south of Cermak Road. Fifty years ago there was nothing south of Cermak but factories; now there's merely nothing. And speaking of urban decay, there *is* substantial gang activity throughout the neighborhood so keep both your eyes peeled.

If you like a decidedly urban edge, spectacular views of the loop, and cheap rents, you should check out Pilsen. Just be prepared to move in a few years if your financial lot has not kept pace with the neighborhood's upward trend.

**Area Code:** 312

**Zip Codes:** 60608, 60616

**Post Office:** Pilsen, 1859 South Ashland Avenue, 312-733-1156; Twenty-Second, 2035 South State, 312-225-9110

**Police District:** 12th/Monroe District (Area 4), 100 South Racine Avenue, 312-746-8396

**Emergency Hospitals:** Cook County Hospital, 1835 West Harrison Street, 312-633-6000; Mercy Hospital and Medical Center, 2525 South Michigan Avenue, 312-567-2000; Rush-Presbyterian St. Luke's Hospital, 1653 West Congress Parkway, 312-942-5000; University of Illinois Hospital and Clinics, 1740 West Taylor Street, 312-996-9634

**Library:** Lozano, 1805 South Loomis Street, 312-746-4329

**Transportation - Rapid Transit:** Blue (*O'Hare/Congress/Douglas*) Line (stations: 18th, Hoyne)

**Transportation - Major Bus Routes:** #8 Halsted, #9 Ashland, #18 16th-18th, #21 Cermak, #50 Damen, #60 Blue Island

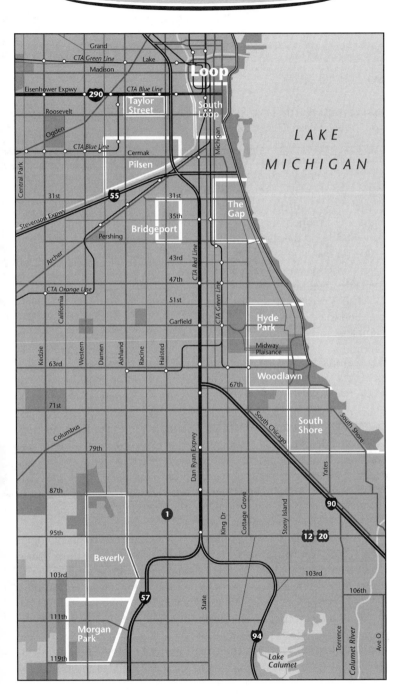

## SOUTH

## SOUTH LOOP

**Boundaries: North:** Jackson Boulevard; **East:** Lake Shore Drive; **South:** 16th Street; **West:** Chicago River.

The South Loop has been developing steadily since the early 1980s and continues to enjoy a construction boom. Most recently, and most exciting is the Lake Shore Drive Improvement Project. In 1997 the city moved Lake Shore Drive's northbound lanes west of Soldier Field and the Field Museum; a monumental task to say the least. That created ten acres of park land along the shore and was completed with elegant landscaping, including bike and foot paths. New bridges and walkways connect the neighborhoods west of Lake Shore Drive to this new park area, as well as the 18th Street Metra stop.

This is great news for the South Loop area. Interestingly, the neighborhood is located in what a century ago was Chicago's most notorious gambling and prostitution district, prompting a U.S. Senator to refer to Chicago as the "Gomorrah of the West." Like the Biblical reference, no traces of the First Ward in that era remain. Today the South Loop consists of three established neighborhoods — Dearborn Park, Printers Row and River City — and other nearby developments. A new neighborhood, dubbed Central Station, is being developed east of Michigan Avenue and south of Roosevelt Road across Lake Shore Drive from the Field Museum.

**Dearborn Park** (312-326-3730) is a 15-year-old townhouse and condominium development built on land formerly owned by several railroads. It lies directly south of the Loop between State Street and Clark Street, south of Polk Street to 15th Street. New, beautiful and expensive single-family homes are being built to the south of the original high-rise and town house development.

**Printers Row** is a condominium and rental area in loft buildings located just south of the Loop. Restaurants, bars and book stores abound, and every May/June the neighborhood hosts a large book fair. If you work in the Loop and want to be close to the office, few locations are more convenient or architectually attractive.

A little further south, the **River City** (312-431-2800) apartments-only complex boasts outstanding views of the Loop and has docking facilities for 70 boats on the south branch of the Chicago River. Developed in the mid-1980s, River City is a city within a city containing a health club, restaurants and other amenities.

**Central Station** (312-920-7440) is a promising new development. The $2 billion, 72-acre project is home to Mayor Richard M. Daley and his family, who moved there from their longtime South Side home in the Bridgeport neighborhood. With 180 homes under construction, its proximity to the lovely expanded green spaces surrounding Soldier Field, the Field Museum and the Adler Planetarium, and with the Mayor as a neighbor, you can bet these digs are swanky and only for the well-heeled. Developers are also planning office and retail space.

And if that's not enough, you may sleep easier at night knowing that the South Loop lies in the shadow of the Sears Tower, still the nation's, if not the world's, tallest building. Who says totem worship doesn't still exist?

**Area Code:** 312

**Zip Codes:** 60604, 60605, 60606, 60607

**Post Offices:** Main Post Office, 433 West Harrison Street, 765-4357; Loop Station, 211 South Clark Street, 427-4225; 22nd Street, 2035 South State Street, 225-9110

**Police District:** 1st/Central District (Area 1), 1121 South State Street, 747-6230

**Emergency Hospital:** University of Illinois Hospital and Clinics, 1740 West Taylor Street, 996-7000; Mercy Hospital and Medical Center, 2525 South Michigan Avenue, 567-2000

**Libraries:** Harold Washington Library, 400 South State Street, 747-4300

**Transportation - Rapid Transit:** Red (*Howard/Dan Ryan*) Line (stations: Jackson, Harrison, Roosevelt); Brown (*Ravenswood*) Line (station: Library); Green (*Lake/Englewood/Jackson Park*) Line (station: Adams-Wabash); Blue (*O'Hare/Congress/Douglas*) Line (stations: Jackson, LaSalle); Orange (*Midway*) Line (stations: Roosevelt, Library)

**Transportation - Main Bus Routes:** #3 King Drive, #4 Cottage Grove, #12 Roosevelt, #22 Clark, #24 Wentworth, #29 State, #36 Broadway, #62 Archer

## THE GAP

**Boundaries: North:** 26th Street; **East:** Lake Michigan; **South:** 39th Street; **West:** Michigan Avenue

The Gap is a near South Side neighborhood that is a mixture of high-rise developments such as South Commons and original Victorian greystones and brownstones. The neighborhood earned its name years ago when it literally was the gap between Chinatown on the north and De LaSalle High School on the south.

Groveland Park, which lies between 33rd and 35th Streets near Lake Michigan, is a remnant of Senator Stephen A. Douglas' once large land-holdings in the area. Douglas, who ran against Abraham Lincoln for president in 1860, mistakenly believed that Chicago's commercial development would focus closer to the mouth of the Calumet River near 95th Street and not along the Chicago River. Although he was forced to mortgage the property in 1851, it wasn't developed until 1873 after Douglas' sons won a series of lawsuits and established a homeowners association to keep up the public lands. While many of the earlier homes are gone, some highly altered versions of the first buildings still exist facing the park. This area is also known as Douglas after its famous early promoter.

The Gap once was a wealthy and predominantly Jewish area filled with street after street of Victorian row houses, some of them designed by Louis Sullivan and Frank Lloyd Wright. The area fell on hard times for many years, but now it's making a strong comeback as professionals, many of them African-American, are picking up the run-down greystones at bargain-basement prices and rehabbing them to their former glory.

Driving south on Dr. Martin Luther King Jr. Drive, the contrast between old and new is remarkable. From 26th Street to 35th street, the new developments tower overhead but they are surrounded by large open spaces. South of 35th you feel like you've stepped back one hundred years. The houses are spectacular, with intricate stonework and wrought iron fences, a perfect complement to this wide, tree-lined boulevard.

A word of caution to the newcomer, this neighborhood is still a bit edgy in terms of safety. Visit the neighborhood and walk the streets before moving here; it's the best way to determine your own comfort level with an area.

**Area Codes:** 312 and 773

**Zip Codes:** 60616, 60653

**Post Offices:** Twenty-Second Street, 2035 South State Street, 312-225-9110; Hyde Park, 4601 South Cottage Grove Avenue, 773-924-9221

**Police Districts:** North of 35th Street and east of Cottage Grove Avenue: 21st/Prairie District (Area 1), 300 East 29th Street, 312-747-8340; south of 35th Street and west of Cottage Grove: 2nd/Wentworth District (Area 1), 5101 South Wentworth Avenue, 312-747-8366

**Emergency Hospitals:** Mercy Hospital and Medical Center, 2525 South Michigan Avenue, 312-567-2000; Michael Reese Hospital & Medical Center, 2929 South Ellis Avenue, 312-791-2000

**Library:** King, 3436 South King Drive, 312-747-7543

**Transportation - Rapid Transit:** Green (*Lake/Englewood/Jackson Park*) Line (stations: 35, Bronzeville, IIT); Metra/Electric Line (station: 27th Street)

**Transportation - Major Bus Routes:** #1 Indiana/Hyde Park, #3 King Drive, #4 Cottage Grove, #35 35th Street, #39 Pershing

## BRIDGEPORT

**Boundaries: North:** 31st Street; **East:** Canal Street; **South:** 39th Street; **West:** Morgan Street

Bridgeport is a fine old Chicago neighborhood. It is filled with single-family bungalows and two- and three-flats; real-estate prices within the last decade have risen dramatically for a middle-income neighborhood well away from the lake. Nevertheless, for what you get, Bridgeport is still a relatively affordable area for renters and first-time home buyers.

Perhaps best known as the one-time home of both Mayor Daleys, Bridgeport has been a bastion of Irish-Catholic movers and shakers since it was first settled by Irish immigrants in the 19th century. Mayor Richard J. Daley's widow, Eleanor, still lives in a neighborhood bungalow, but her son has departed for the tonier Central Station neighborhood in the South Loop (see profile above).

Bridgeport is a world unto itself, a residential island surrounded by factories, railroad tracks, and expressways. The world-famous Chicago stockyards lie just south of here. They provided the inspiration and the material for Upton Sinclair's classic exposé of the meat-packing industry, *The Jungle*.

Bridgeport is no jungle these days, though it remains insular and maybe a little provincial (it's not unusual for residents to live within a few doors of the house where they grew up). Names on Bridgeport mailboxes, though, are changing along with the city as more Asian and Hispanic families make this family-friendly neighborhood their own.

There are no Cubs fans in Bridgeport, or at least none who will admit it, since the new Comiskey Park, home of the Chicago White Sox on the banks of the Dan Ryan Expressway, lies within walking distance of the neighborhood. New housing is being erected in the vicinity of Comiskey Park. Like Wrigleyville, parking regulations are strictly enforced during night games.

**Area Codes:** 312 and 773

**Zip Codes:** 60608, 60609, 60616

**Post Office:** Stockyards, 4101 South Halsted Street, 773-247-6901

**Police District:** 9th/Deering District (Area 3), 3501 South Lowe Avenue, 312-747-8227

**Emergency Hospitals:** Mercy Hospital and Medical Center, 2525 South Michigan Avenue, 312-567-2000; Michael Reese Hospital & Medical Center, 2929 South Ellis Avenue, 312-791-2000

**Library:** Daley, 3400 South Halsted Street, 312-747-8990

**Transportation - Rapid Transit:** Red (*Howard/Dan Ryan*) Line (stations: Sox/35th)

**Transportation - Major Bus Routes:** #8 Halsted, #35 35th Street, #39 Pershing, #44 Wallace/Racine

## HYDE PARK

**Boundaries: North:** 51st Street; **East:** Lake Michigan; **South:** 60th Street; **West:** Cottage Grove Avenue

Thanks to the University of Chicago, Hyde Park is a bastion of cosmopolitan culture, which makes it something of an anomaly on the otherwise unpolished South Side. Although the area is surrounded by poor neighborhoods, Hyde Park prides itself on being one of the few truly (racially)

integrated neighborhoods in Chicago. The University of Chicago police, which was once the second largest force in the state of Illinois, helps Chicago Police patrol the neighborhood. It should be stressed, however, that crime is a problem in some of the less-affluent bordering areas.

Hyde Park was the site of the World Columbian Exposition of 1893, celebrating the 400th anniversary of the (re)discovery of America. The reconstructed Museum of Science and Industry is the only surviving building from that enormous event. The neighborhood is filled with architectural jewels, including Frank Lloyd Wright's famous Robie House. Grand old high-rise apartment buildings line the lakefront, and away from the lake the neighborhood is chock-a-block with low-rise apartments, many of which have become condominiums. Rents and real-estate prices are not cheap here although prices do drop the closer you move to the edges of the neighborhood. As befits an area with one of the country's leading universities, there are several first-rate book stores, including and especially The Seminary Co-op and Powell's.

With all of the university activity going on in Hyde Park, it is easy to overlook the quiet elegance of Hyde Park's northerly neighbor, **Kenwood**. The southern end of Kenwood (referred to as "South Kenwood" by residents) lies between 51st and 47th Streets, running east to Lake Michigan, and west to Cottage Grove Avenue. It's a small neighborhood with old estates on large lots. The last ten years has seen the development of lovely new townhouses as well as new businesses on 47th Street. Kenwood is worth looking into if you like quiet shaded streets, large old homes and university access.

**Area Code:** 773

**Zip Codes:** 60615, 60637

**Post Offices:** Hyde Park, 4601 South Cottage Grove Avenue, 773-924-9221; U, 956 East 58th Street, 773-324-2723

**Police District:** 21st/Prairie District (Area 1), 300 East 29th Street, 312-747-8340

**Emergency Hospitals:** Hyde Park Hospital, 5800 South Stony Island Avenue, 773-643-9200; The University of Chicago Hospitals, 5841 South Maryland Avenue, 773-702-1000

**Library:** Blackstone, 4904 South Lake Park Avenue, 312-747-0511

**Transportation - Rapid Transit:** Metra/Electric Line (stations: 47th Street, 51st Street, 55th Street, 59th Street)

**Transportation - Major Bus Routes:** #1 Indiana/Hyde Park, #2 Hyde Park Express, #4 Cottage Grove, #6 Jeffery Express, #28 Stony Island, #47 47th Street, #51 51st Street, #55 Garfield.

## WOODLAWN

**Boundaries: North:** 59th Street; **East:** Lake Michigan; **South:** 67th Street; **West:** Cottage Grove Avenue

Just south of Hyde Park lies Woodlawn, an African-American neighborhood in the process of revitalizing itself through independent initiatives led by a local Baptist church, private investors and groups like WECAN (Woodlawn East Community And Neighbors) and Renaissance. WECAN works to renovate the area's low-income flats, rebuilding them into affordable, attractive apartments for families or singles; Renaissance has already built and opened nearly 120 units of moderately priced housing. As a result, professionals as well as working class families have begun to relocate to Woodlawn. The recent opening of two banks (branches of the Cole Taylor Bank and First Chicago) in the area has also helped to attract businesses.

Close to the University of Chicago, Woodlawn is also within walking distance of Jackson Park to the east and Washington Park to the west. The colossal Museum of Science and Industry is nearby as well. Residents enjoy the proximity to Hyde Park's retail district, although several small grocery stores have served the neighborhood for over 50 years.

Safety is definitely a concern in Woodlawn, and an investigative visit (especially in the evening) is recommended before moving here.

**Area Code:** 773

**Zip Code:** 60637

**Post Office:** Jackson Park Post Office, 700 East 61st Street, 773-493-3124

**Police District:** Third District (Area 2), 7040 South Cottage Grove Avenue, 312-747-8201

**Emergency Hospitals:** Hyde Park Hospital, 5800 South Stony Island Avenue, 773-643-9200; The University of Chicago Hospitals, 5841 South Maryland Avenue, 773-702-1000

**Library:** Bessie Coleman, 731 East 63rd Street, 312-747-7770

**Transportation - Rapid Transit:** Green (*Lake/Jackson*) Line (station: Cottage Grove); Metra/Electric Line (stations: 59th Street, 63rd Street)

**Transportation - Major Bus Routes:** #4 Cottage Grove, #28 Stony Island, #59 59th - 61st Street, #63 63rd Street

## SOUTH SHORE

**Boundaries: North:** 67th Street; **East:** Lake Michigan; **South:** 79th Street; **West:** Stony Island Avenue

Extending from the base of Jackson Park to 79th Street, South Shore is a study in contrasts. Many working professionals live along the park, attracted by the convenience of the commute downtown: South Shore is served by the Metra South Shore Line and Lake Shore Drive begins here. Artists live here too (though perhaps not on the park) attracted by cheaper rents and local theater companies.

The population is predominantly African-American but economically divided. Immediately south of the park the apartments and high rises are well maintained, but they tend to get more rundown the further one moves south along the lakeshore. Inland there are blighted areas, but again these are balanced by immaculate middle and upper middle class residential streets. Numerous urban redevelopment projects have been undertaken to revitalize the community.

Jackson Park, at the neighborhood's northern edge, is a beautiful lakeshore park with inland lagoons and a golf course. Just to the south is the landmark South Shore Cultural Center. Built as an elite country club at the turn of the century, it was acquired by the Chicago Park District in the 1970s and now offers daily classes in the performing arts as well as a full schedule of concerts, lectures, and plays. Call 312-747-2536 for more information.

**Area Code:** 773

**Zip Code:** 60649

**Post Office:** South Shore, 2207 East 57th Street, 773-375-4022

**Police District:** 3rd/Grand Crossing District (Area 2), 7040 South Cottage Grove Avenue, 312-747-8201

**Emergency Hospitals:** Jackson Park Hospital, 7531 South Stony

Island Avenue, 773-947-7500; St. Bernard Hospital, 64th Street and Dan Ryan Expressway, 773-962-3900; South Shore Hospital, 8012 South Crandon Avenue, 773-768-0810

**Library:** South Shore, 2505 East 73rd Street, 312-747-5281

**Transportation - Rapid Transit:** Metra/Electric South Chicago Branch Line (stations: 75th Street, Stony Island, Bryn Mawr, South Shore, Windsor Park, Cheltenham)

**Transportation - Major Bus Routes:** #6 Jeffery Local, #27 South Deering, #28 Stony Island, #67 67th-69th-91st, #71 71st, #75 74th-75th, #79 79th.

## BEVERLY

**Boundaries: North:** 87th Street; **East:** Beverly Avenue to 103rd Street and Vincennes Avenue to 107th Street; **South:** 107th Street; **West:** Western Avenue

The Gold Coast of the South Side, Beverly is one of the most affluent neighborhoods in Chicago. Huge old mansions, including a Frank Lloyd Wright, line the top of Longwood Drive (which was the edge of Lake Michigan about 10,000 years ago and one of the highest points geographically in Chicago). The most exclusive section, North Beverly, between 89th Street and 94th Street, features many large, Revival-style houses built in the 1920s and 1930s on hilly lots. The first homes in the area date from the mid-19th century before Beverly was incorporated into Chicago. Although once predominantly Irish-Catholic, the neighborhood is integrating successfully and remains a stable, desirable place to live. Apartment seekers should note that Beverly is primarily a neighborhood of single-family residences, though there are a handful of apartment buildings in the neighborhood.

**Area Code:** 773

**Zip Codes:** 60620, 60643

**Post Office:** Morgan Park, 1805 West Monterey Avenue, 773-238-3441

**Police District:** 22nd/Morgan Park District (Area 2), 1830 West Monterey Avenue, 312-747-6381

**Emergency Hospital:** Little Company of Mary Hospital, 2800 West

95th Street, Evergreen Park, 708-422-6200

**Library:** Beverly, 2121 West 95th Street, 312-747-9673; Woodson Regional, 9525 South Halsted Street, 312-747-6900

**Transportation - Rapid Transit:** Metra/Rock Island Suburban Line (91st Street; 95th Street; 99th Street; 103rd Street; 107th Street)

**Transportation - Major Bus Routes:** #49 Western, #87 87th Street, #95 95th Street, #112 Vincennes/111th

## MORGAN PARK

**Boundaries: North:** 107th Street; **East:** South Vincennes Avenue; **South:** 119th Street; **West:** California Avenue

Hills? Winding streets? Can this be Chicago? Morgan Park may induce a panic attack in those who have grown accustomed to flat-as-a-pancake, straight-as-an-arrow Chicago driving. None of the rules hold here, and you can be forgiven for thinking that you've somehow wandered into a suburb. At this distance from downtown (fifteen miles as the crow flies), the distinction between urban and suburban is a technicality.

Morgan Park is a quiet residential neighborhood with old trees and big lawns. Single-family homes make up the majority of the housing stock, though there are some condos by the Metra stations. Residents here aren't ashamed of their luck. Morgan Park (much like its northern neighbor, Beverly) offers all the perks of the city with few of the drawbacks.

While Morgan Park is technically part of the Beverly Area Planning Association (BAPA), a local neighbors group, there are differences between the two neighborhoods. Beverly is more affluent and the houses more expensive. Also, Morgan Park has those funky winding streets which slow you down when driving and let you appreciate the scenery. If you'd like to get a more detailed look at both neighborhoods, BAPA puts out a brochure called "Biking Around Beverly Hills/Morgan Park" which maps out a nine mile tour. Call them at 773-233-3100.

**Area Code:** 773

**Zip Codes:** 60643, 60655

**Post Office:** Morgan Park, 1805 West Monterey Avenue, 773-238-3441

**Police District:** 22nd/Morgan Park District (Area 2), 1830 West Monterey Avenue, 312-747-6381

**Emergency Hospitals:** Little Company of Mary Hospital, 2800 West 95th Street, Evergreen Park, 708-422-6200; Roseland Community Hospital, 45 West 111th Street, 773-995-3000

**Library:** Beverly, 2121 West 95th Street, 312-747-9673; Mount Greenwood, 11010 South Kedzie Avenue, 312-747-2805

**Transportation - Rapid Transit:** Metra/Rock Island Suburban Line (107th Street; 111th Street; 115th Street; 119th Street)

**Transportation - Major Bus Routes:** #49A South Western, #111 Pullman/111th/115th, #112 Vincennes/111th, #119 Michigan/119th

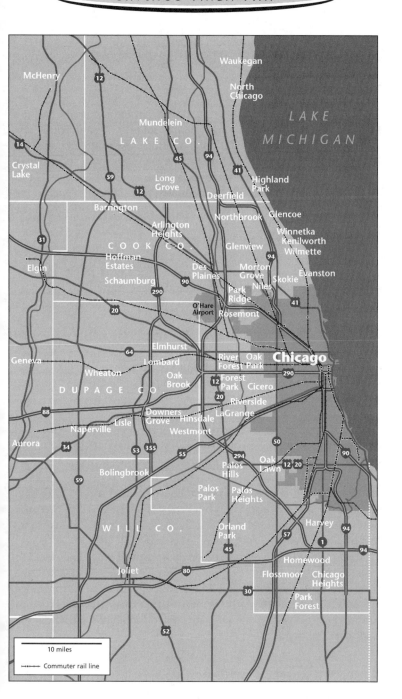

LAKE MICHIGAN

McHenry

Waukegan

North Chicago

Mundelein

LAKE CO.

Crystal Lake

Long Grove

Highland Park

Deerfield

Barrington

Northbrook

Glencoe

Arlington Heights

Winnetka
Kenilworth
Wilmette

COOK CO.

Glenview

Hoffman Estates

Des Plaines

Morton Grove

Skokie

Evanston

Elgin

Schaumburg

Park Ridge

Niles

O'Hare Airport

Rosemont

Elmhurst

Geneva

River Forest

Oak Park

Chicago

Lombard

Wheaton

Oak Brook

Forest Park

Cicero

DUPAGE CO.

Riverside

Downers Grove

Hinsdale

LaGrange

Naperville

Lisle

Westmont

Aurora

Oak Lawn

Palos Hills

Bolingbrook

Palos Park

Palos Heights

WILL CO.

Orland Park

Harvey

Homewood

Flossmoor

Chicago Heights

Joliet

Park Forest

10 miles

Commuter rail line

## SUBURBS

### EVANSTON

The first jewel in the North Shore necklace, Evanston is one of Chicago's oldest, most prestigious and most beautiful suburbs. It's a thriving community with a well-developed shopping district, lakefront parks and, last but not least, Northwestern University. The mansions lining either side of Sheridan Road will take your breath away. The extensive network of biking paths, running trails, and beaches along the shoreline will do the same, both figuratively and literally. Although the lakeshore area is the only part of Evanston that many people see, it should be noted that not all of the neighborhoods are as spectacular.

Evanston's downtown shopping area and the quaint Central Street are a mix of chain stores and small businesses and the ample, low-cost parking is a refreshing change from high-priced garages in the Loop. Heading south along Chicago Avenue you will eventually cross over Dempster Street, and then Main Street. Both of these are home to a cluster of small shops, restaurants, and coffee shops. You will be relieved by the lack of panhandlers in shopping areas. In 1994 the city enacted an innovative initiative urging residents not to give money to beggars; businesses contribute to a separate program that provides food and clothing to those in need.

Actually the sixth largest city in the state, Evanston's population of 80,000 runs the gamut, and its neighborhoods extend west to Crawford Street and the North Shore Channel. A bustling office park near Northwestern University has brought more business to the community and the quick Evanston Express commuter train offers direct transportation to and from the Loop during rush hours; the Metra commuter train is even faster and more spacious but runs less frequently. The Evanston Express can be boarded at any "L" station (in Evanston) and the Metra station's are at Central Street, Davis Street and Main Street.

If you like nightlife, even in moderation, you'll be heading down to Chicago frequently. The few bars that are here are bland and slow-paced. Evanston was once home to the Women's Christian Temperance movement, and even with the youthful student population of Northwestern University, the long shadow of Prohibition somehow still hangs over the city.

**Area Code:** 847

**Zip Codes:** 60201, 60202, 60204

**Post Offices:** Main Post Office, 1101 Davis Street, 60204, 328-6201; South Station Branch, 701 Main Street, 328-6201; North Station Branch, 1929 Central Street, 328-6201

**Police:** Evanston Police Department, 1454 Elmwood Street, 866-5000

**Emergency Hospitals:** Evanston Hospital, 2650 Ridge Avenue, Evanston, 570-2000; St. Francis Hospital of Evanston, 355 Ridge Avenue, Evanston, 316-4000

**Libraries:** Evanston Public Library, 1703 Orrington (entrance on Church Street), 866-0300; North Branch Public Library, 2026 Central, 866-0330; South Branch Public Library, 949 Chicago Avenue, 866-0333

**Transportation - Rapid Transit:** Evanston Express Purple Line (stations: South Boulevard, Main, Dempster, Davis, Foster, Noyes, Central). Metra/Union Pacific North Line (stations: Main, Davis, Central)

**Transportation - Major Bus Routes:** #215 Howard, #97 Oakton, #250 Dempster, #208 Church, #212 Golf, #202 Main/Emerson, #213 Green Bay Road, #201 Central/Sherman, #203 Ridge, #204 Dodge

## SKOKIE

Skokie, Evanston's neighbor to the west, is a village of 60,000 that incorporated almost 100 years ago. In 1940, the name was changed from Niles Center to Skokie, a Native American word for swamp. An agricultural and greenhouse center for years, its main settlers emigrated from Germany, Switzerland and Luxembourg. Known as a western settlement in the early part of the century, film studios once used the village's unpretentious main street to film cowboy movies. After World War II, large numbers of Jewish refugees settled in Skokie, and the village remains family- and religion-oriented, with many churches and synagogues. More recently, Skokie's attractiveness to immigrants has not diminished as newcomers from Korea, Malaysia, India and Russia have decided to make Skokie home.

Much of the village consists of single-family homes, although there are some condominiums and apartment buildings scattered throughout. The community has done a good job of combining family programs and an interest in the arts; Skokie's Centre East Performing Arts Center has an active youth theater and the village also has its own symphony, The SkokieValley Symphony Orchestra. It's also home to the new North Shore Center for the Performing Arts. The park district boasts a nine-hole golf course, an ice skating rink, and almost 200 acres of park land and swimming pools. The Skokie Historical Society organizes tours and publishes a chronicle of the village's early days, which includes the history of the circa-1887 fire station (now a museum) and other buildings included on the National Registry.

Skokie has established itself as a suburban shopper's paradise. The shops on Dempster Street and the recently revamped Old Orchard Mall make the community the eighth largest retail center in the state.

**Area Code:** 847

**Zip Codes:** 60076, 60077

**Post Office:** 4950 Madison Street, 676-2200

**Police:** Skokie Police Department, 8350 Laramie Avenue, 982-5900

**Emergency Hospitals:** Rush North Shore Medical Center, 9600 Gross Point Road, 677-9600; St. Francis Health Center, 7126 Lincoln Avenue, Lincolnwood, 675-2273

**Library:** Skokie Public Library, 5215 Oakton Street, 673-7774

**Transportation - Rapid Transit:** Skokie Swift Yellow Line (Skokie station)

**Transportation - Major Bus Routes:** #97 (Skokie station)

## WILMETTE

The lake shore village of Wilmette, just north of Evanston, is an affluent suburb (median family income is nearly $100,000 a year) of approximately 27,000 residents. Bordering the lake, it is a community that is best known for its tree-lined streets and large, expensive homes, some of which have been converted into apartments or condominiums. Besides the expansive, impeccably manicured lawns and homes, one way to tell when you have passed from Evanston into Wilmette is the brick streets of the neighborhood, which residents have fought to keep over the years. The village is run by a president and board of trustees, employing 210 full-time employees (including a village nurse).

Wilmette's prosperous homogeneity gives it a crime rate less than half that of many Chicago North Side neighborhoods. For weekday commuters it is a fairly easy drive or train ride into the city. Known as the place where many Evanston residents move when they have outgrown a first apartment or home, Wilmette's real estate prices reflect its exclusivity. Wilmette's neighboring suburbs of **Kenilworth, Winnetka**, and **Glencoe** are even more well-to-do.

Wilmette is the home of Baha'i Temple, a gleaming white-domed building which is situated on Sheridan Road across from Lake Michigan. This beautiful (and incongruous on the suburban North Shore) sight is worth stopping for if you're just passing through.

Kenilworth Realty Co, 847-251-5600, handles properties in Wilmette and other North Shore areas.

**Area Code:** 847

**Zip Code:** 60091

**Post Office:** 1241 Central Avenue, 251-8644

**Police:** Wilmette Police Department, 710 Ridge Road, 256-1200

**Emergency Hospitals:** Evanston Hospital, 2650 Ridge Avenue, Evanston, 570-2000; Rush North Shore Medical Center, 9600 Gross Point Road, 677-9600

**Library:** Wilmette Public Library, 1242 Wilmette Avenue, 256-5025

**Transportation - Rapid Transit:** Evanston Express Purple Line (Linden Street station), Metra/Union Pacific North Line (Wilmette)

# NORTHBROOK

The village of Northbrook is located twenty-three miles to the northwest of downtown Chicago. Originally incorporated as Shermerville in 1901, the village adopted the current name in 1923. Northbrook is very commuter-friendly, with its own Metra station and instant access to both the Edens Expressway (I-94) and the Tri-State Tollway (I-294). Northbrook is also an excellent place to raise a family. The neighborhoods here are quiet and residential; the Northbrook Park District has tennis courts, two swimming pools, a golf course, indoor ice arenas, and even a velodrome; single-family homes account for more than 75 percent of the housing stock; the village population is slightly over thirty thousand; the local schools are excellent. But you may have trouble affording it — in 1996 the average home price was $320,000.

Northbrook's most prominent architectural landmark is probably Northbrook Court. The first of Chicago's luxury malls (an oxymoron perhaps, but a very successful one), Northbrook Court is home to Lord & Taylor, Neiman Marcus, I. Magnin and other blue-chip retailers. This is where power shoppers come to flex their platinum cards.

Northbrook offers a lot to its residents, and is one of the most sought-after addresses in the Chicago area. The good news is, even if you can't afford to live here, you can pretend to shop here.

**Area Code:** 847

**Zip Code:** 60062

**Post Offices:** Main Post Office, 2460 Dundee Road, 272-0018; Downtown Station, 1157 Church Street, 480-1511

**Police:** 1225 Cedar Lane, 564-2060 (Non-Emergency) and 911 (Emergency)

**Emergency Hospitals:** Highland Park Hospital, 718 Glenview Avenue, Highland Park, 432-8000; Glenbrook Hospital, 2100 Pfingsten Road, Glenview, 657-5800

**Library:** Northbrook Public Library, 1201 Cedar Lane, 272-6224

**Transportation:** Metra/Milwaukee District North Line (Northbrook station)

## DEERFIELD

The village of Deerfield lies just north of Northbrook, next to the Tri-State Tollway. Home prices are slightly less expensive here (the average price was $270,000 in 1996) and Deerfield offers the same family-friendly features as its southern neighbor. These are: easy access to car or train commuting, an excellent public school system, a variety of smaller residential areas to choose from, and an extensive system of parks and recreational facilities. In short, Deerfield is indeed a proverbial "great place to raise kids."

Though located at the southern edge of Lake County, Deerfield is close to the Chicago Botanic Garden and the North Branch Bicycle Trail (see the "Green Spaces" chapter for more information on both). It's also close to the famous Ravinia Park, which is located in the neighboring suburb of **Highland Park**. Ravinia (847-266-5100) offers a summer-long series of open-air concerts (ranging from classical to folk and jazz) with much of the seating outside on the grass. People bring blankets and elaborate picnics and dine *al fresco* to the music of Mozart and Bach — it's all very refined and very fun.

On a more raucous note, professional basketball fans may be interested to know that Deerfield is home to the Berto Center, the Chicago Bulls' practice facility, as well as the homes of several players and coaches. There is good shopping, and major local employers include Walgreens and Baxter. The Deerfield Park District manages over 21 parks and playgrounds, as well as two swimming pools, and every type of playing field or sports facility you can imagine.

**Area Code:** 847

**Zip Code:** 60015

**Post Office:** 707 Osterman Avenue, 945-0257

**Police:** 850 North Waukegan Road, 945-8636 (Non-Emergency) and 911 (Emergency)

**Emergency Hospital:** Highland Park Hospital, 718 Glenview Avenue, Highland Park, 432-8000

**Library:** Deerfield Public Library, 920 North Waukegan Road, 945-3311 (TDD 945-3372)

**Transportation:** Metra/Milwaukee District North Line (Deerfield station)

## ROSEMONT

Lying only five minutes from O'Hare International Airport and about 30 minutes from the Loop, the small (population 4000) village of Rosemont was initially established as more of an industrial park, offering support to the airport and nearby office parks. The same mayor, Donald E. Stephens, has been in office since the village incorporated, in 1956, when the place consisted of little more than truck farms (where vegetables were grown and then driven into the city) and several sparsely populated subdivisions. When O'Hare International Airport was built, both the Northwest Tollway and the Tri-State Tollway soon followed, making the village a convenient stop-off and eventually a convention destination. Not surprisingly, many of the residents work in one of the office parks, at the Convention Center or in the adjacent restaurants, hotels and retail shops. In 1976, a former factory was converted into the Rosemont Convention Center, the tenth-largest meeting space in the country. In addition, the Rosemont Horizon indoor stadium regularly hosts the Ringling Brothers and Barnum & Bailey Circus, DePaul University basketball and the Chicago Wolves, an International Hockey League team.

**Area Code:** 847

**Zip Codes:** 60018, 60019

**Post Office:** Rosemont Post Office, 6153 Gage Street (drop-off only, no phone)

**Police:** Rosemont Police Department, 9501 Devon Avenue, 823-1134

**Emergency Hospital:** Holy Family Hospital, 100 North River Road, Des Plaines, 297-1800

**Library:** Des Plaines Public Library, 841 Graceland Avenue, 827-5551

**Transportation - Rapid Transit:** Blue (*O'Hare/Congress/Douglas*) Line (Rosemont station)

## DES PLAINES

A much older and larger village northwest of the city (but inside Cook County), Des Plaines may be best known as the birthplace of McDonald's. McDonald's Original Restaurant and Museum is probably the village's biggest tourist attraction. Founded in 1835, Des Plaines was named for its location along the river of the same name and consisted of truck farms and factories before the construction of O'Hare International Airport. It was incorporated in 1869.

Most of its 50,000 plus residents make a daily commute into the city via the Metra/Union Pacific rail or Tri-State Tollway, about a 30-minute trip to the Loop (notwithstanding rush hours). Thirty-seven beautiful parks include the 73-acre Lake Park, which offers boating, a golf course and spacious picnic spots. Large shopping centers, malls and excellent schools add to the bucolic suburban atmosphere. Although rental properties are somewhat limited, apartments are affordable. According to the Des Plaines Chamber of Commerce, the median rent in 1996 was $725.

**Area Code:** 847

**Zip Codes:** 60016, 60017, 60018, 60019

**Post Office:** 1000 East Oakton Street, 827-5591

**Police:** Des Plaines Police Department, 1420 Miner Street, 391-5400

**Emergency Hospitals:** Holy Family Hospital, 100 North River Road, 297-1800; Lutheran General Hospital, 1775 Dempster Street, Park Ridge, 723-2210

**Library:** Des Plaines Public Library, 841 Graceland Avenue, 827-5551

**Transportation - Rapid Transit:** Metra/Union Pacific Northwest Line (stations: Des Plaines, Minor and Lee Streets, and Cumberland, Golf Road and Northwest Highway)

## OAK PARK

One of Oak Park's famous sons, Ernest Hemingway, is said to have described this western suburb as a community of wide lawns and narrow minds. The wide lawns (and avenues) remain, but not the narrow minds. Oak Park today is a vibrant community whose progressive policies provided for controlled integration rather than the white flight that has plagued other suburbs. It was also the first municipality in Illinois to offer same-sex domestic partner benefits to city employees. The village is filled with architectural landmarks, including Frank Lloyd Wright's long-time home and studio, as well as his Unity Temple, and many residences designed by the master.

Oak Park is divided by the Eisenhower Expressway. You'll notice that the ramps at Austin and Harlem enter and exit on the left; residents didn't want Oak Park cut up any more than necessary. Generally, the area south of the expressway is more affordable. This also holds true for those areas which border the Chicago city line.

If you want to live near the city, but not in it, Oak Park is a good choice. The downtown is quaint, with a small town feel to it, and there are several good shopping areas throughout the village. Many of the streets are beautiful, with attractive houses and huge old trees. It's also a convenient place to live if you work in the city: two CTA train lines run through the community, Metra has a station here, and the expressway is always near at hand. Finally, for a suburb, Oak Park is quite affordable — the average price of a single-family home in 1996 was just under $200,000.

If you do decide to live here, parking can be a problem, especially if you have guests. There is no street parking allowed between 2:30 a.m. and 6 a.m. in Oak Park. Visitors can park on the street, but only if you notify the Oak Park Police and give them the car's license plate number. As a new resident, you receive a 30-day pass from the parking office to park on the street. After that, you can buy a sticker and park overnight in village lots. For more information, call the Oak Park Village parking department at 383-6400, ext. 236.

**Area Code:** 708

**Zip Codes:** 60301, 60302, 60304

**Post Offices:** Main Station, 901 Lake Street, 848-7900; South Station, 917 South Oak Park Avenue, 848-6464

**Police:** Oak Park Police, One Village Hall Plaza (Lombard and Madison), 386-3800

**Emergency Hospitals:** Oak Park Hospital, 520 South Maple Avenue, 383-9300; West Suburban Hospital Medical Center, Erie Street at Austin Boulevard, 287-8100

**Libraries:** Oak Park Main Library, 834 Lake Street, 383-8200; Dole Branch, 255 Augusta Boulevard, 386-9032; Maze Branch, 845 South Gunderson, 386-4751

**Transportation - Rapid Transit:** Lake/Englewood/Jackson Park Green Line (Austin; Ridgeland; Oak Park; Harlem), O'Hare/Congress/Douglas Blue Line (Austin; Oak Park; Harlem; Forest Park), Metra/Union Pacific West Line (Oak Park)

## OTHER SUBURBS

Not everyone who works in Chicago lives in Chicago. Many people are willing to make a longer commute into the city for the pleasure of living in the less-congested suburbs.

Here are some additional suburbs that are attractive places to live outside Chicago:

**North and Northwest:** Arlington Heights; Glencoe; Highland Park; Kenilworth; Morton Grove; Niles; Park Ridge; Winnetka

**West:** Aurora; Forest Park; Hinsdale; LaGrange; Lisle; Lombard; Naperville; Oak Brook; River Forest; Schaumburg; Westmont

**South and Southwest:** Homewood; Flossmoor; Oak Lawn; Orland Park; Palos Heights, Palos Hills and Palos Park

Many suburbs have large, enclosed apartment complexes such as the **International Village** in Lombard and Schaumburg that cater specifically to young singles. Rents at these apartment complexes may be a little higher than if you found a single apartment in that area, but there are social benefits. These complexes sponsor social activities for residents and guests ranging from wintertime billiards tournaments in the recreation center to a poolside keg in summer.

## CHICAGO ADDRESS LOCATOR

It is nearly impossible to get lost in Chicago.

City surveyors laid out Chicago on a grid system, so you don't have to walk more than a block or two to know exactly where you are and how far you are from the Loop.

Chicago's grid system is planned at eight city blocks to the mile with major streets every half mile. Addresses are divided north and south by Madison Street and east and west by State Street. So, if you are standing on the corner of Belmont (3200 North) and Sheffield (1000 West), you are four miles north of Madison and a mile and a half west of State Street.

An exception to this eight-blocks-to-the-mile rule is on the South Side, since the near South Side was an early area of the city to be settled. Although Roosevelt Road is 1200 South by numbers, it is one mile south of Madison. Cermak Road, which is 2200 South, is a mile south of Roosevelt even though its a 10-block count. The next mile comes at 31st Street, even though its nine blocks south of Cermak.

All north-south and east-west streets on the North Side have names. On the South Side, north-south streets have names, except in the southeast part of the city where a few have letters; most east-west streets are numbered, although some have both names and numbers, e.g., 22nd

Street also is Cermak Road, and 39th Street is Pershing Road. The east-west streets are double-numbered, e.g., West 66th Street and a West 66th Place, to represent half blocks. (See diagram below.)

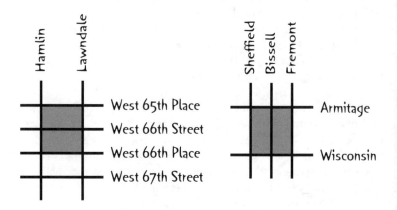

The shaded area represents a full square city block. The distance between West 66th Street and West 66th Place and between Fremont and Bissell is considered a half city block. This is an esoteric point, but one that creates a lot of confusion when trying to give directions and tell people how many blocks away something is.

## APARTMENT HUNTING

I N CHICAGO, FINDING AN APARTMENT YOU LIKE IS NOT AS DIFFICULT as it is in, say, Manhattan or San Francisco; supply and demand seem to be fairly well-aligned in the Windy City. Nevertheless, Chicago has seen nearly two decades of sustained urban renewal as many thousands of former and would-be suburbanites have gravitated back to the diverse and stimulating life of the city. As a result, rents are no longer cheap in many once affordable neighborhoods (Bucktown and Wicker Park, for example). Indeed a recent survey showed Chicago now ranks in the top five most expensive urban areas to rent in the nation.

First, decide how much you can afford to spend on rent. Many people would like to live near Oprah in the Gold Coast, but not everyone can afford it. To gauge your price range, figure on spending no more than 25 to 30 percent of your monthly income on rent.

Once you have calculated how much you can spend on an apartment, you have to decide how much room you need. Odds are that if you're going to live alone, you'll be looking for a one-bedroom apartment or studio. The city is full of them.

Having determined budget limits and space needs, pick a few target neighborhoods. Ask friends and co-workers about where they live. Keep in mind that the money you spend on that Gold Coast efficiency can get you two bedrooms in Rogers Park. You should be aware, however, of some of the facts of Chicago apartment living — the older the building, the smaller the space (including closet space). In places like Ukrainian Village, Bucktown or Wicker Park you will most likely pay extra for space or electric heat. With steam heat, more common in neighborhoods like Andersonville and Rogers Park, the landlord usually pays.

If your funds are limited or you want to live closer to the lake/Loop, consider finding a roommate. A two-bedroom apartment is often not that much more expensive than a one-bedroom, and sometimes a three-bedroom apartment can be shared for the price of two one-bedrooms. If you are new to town and don't know anyone, check "Housing To Share" in Section Four of the *Chicago Reader* for others in search of a roomie.

Once you've narrowed the search down with respect to apartment type, neighborhood, and price range, there are several different ways to start looking.

## HIT THE STREETS

Though perhaps a little low-tech and time-consuming this can be an excellent way to locate apartments. Hop on a bike or get in your car, and drive through your neighborhood of choice.  Keep an eye out for first-floor windows and entryways with bright red or small, black and white "For Rent" signs. Many of these will have the information you need (number of bedrooms and price) to decide whether you want to call the landlord and ask to see the inside. If you're doing this in a car, you might want to bring along a friend who can wait in the car while you're taking down numbers.

This method has some distinct advantages over the classifieds. Many apartments are never advertised in the papers. Building owners who have only one or two apartments will frequently put a sign in the window because they don't want the hassle of advertising in the news-papers. Don't assume that there's any correlation between apartment quality and dollars spent on advertising. Some of the most beautiful and best-kept apartments are hiding behind those cheap plastic signs. Finally, getting a first-hand view of the street, the building and the immediate neighborhood will quickly narrow down your search.

## CLASSIFIEDS

If you have less time and/or energy, peruse the rental listings in the news-papers. The best place to start looking for an apartment in the city is the *Chicago Reader*, a free weekly newspaper that comes out every Thursday night (except the week between Christmas and New Year's). Go to the rentals in Section Four and start circling prospects. If you spot an apartment that you thinkg you might like, don't hesitate to call about it right away because if you don't, dozens of others will. You can subscribe to the *Reader* (11 East Illinois St., Chicago, IL 60611, 312-828-0350) prior to your move to Chicago and learn about the city's housing market in advance. You can also view the *Reader's* valuable classified ad section from your computer by going to *www.chicagoreader.com* (see below for more information).

If you're looking for a place in the suburbs, consult the *Chicago Tribune* (800-TRIBUNE) or the *Chicago Sun-Times* (800-945-5000), both daily newspapers publish large Sunday editions and weekly "home" sections. These newspapers also have apartment listings for the city, but they cover every neighborhood and generally lack the helpful specificity of the add placed in the *Reader*. Another place to look for city apartments is in one of the many local neighborhood papers, such as the *North Loop News* for Gold Coast, Old Town, Lincoln Park and Streeterville. Look for them in vending machines and newsstands in your neighborhood of choice.

## ONLINE

- **Apartment Zone** at *www.apartmentzone.com* is an on-line apartment rental data base for the Chicago area. Apartment searches can be conducted by area, price, and number of bedrooms. Pictures (from inside the apartment and outside the building) are available for each apartment. For more information call 773-489-9000.
- **Chicago Tribune Online** offers online access to the *Tribune's* classified ads and much more. Extensive information on neighborhoods is also available. Go to *www.chicago.tribune.com/homes/*.
- **SpaceFinder** at *www.chicagoreader.com/spacefinder* is the *Chicago Reader's* excellent online database of apartment listings. You'll have a distinct advantage over those who wait for the paper to come out on Thursday because the same listings are available here on Tuesday night.
- **Visual Properties** at *www.apartmentsplus.com* is a nationwide apartment database which offers multiple search modes, pictures of every room, and floor plans. Each entry has an extensive list of building and neighborhood features and you can call to talk to a representative if you want more specifics on individual neighborhoods. Their local address is 1152 N. State Street, 312-397-4212, and if you prefer to deal with a live human being, they will work one-on-one to find you an apartment. Best of all, the landlord pays so there's no fee!

## APARTMENT SEARCH FIRMS

If you don't have enough time, then let someone else do your looking for you. Brokers and real-estate agents often have long lists of apartments for rent and will help you narrow your choice. Many high-rise buildings, and some landlords with extensive holdings, will list vacant apartments with an agent to save themselves the time of having to run around and show them. These services are free to you. The landlord pays the finder's fee, not the renter. Check the Yellow Pages under "Apartments." Here are some popular North Side agencies.

- **The Apartment People**, 3121 North Broadway, 773-248-8800
- **The Apartment Source**, 2638 North Halsted Street, 773-404-9900
- **Relcon Apartment Finders**, 21 West Elm Street, 312-715-5900; Relcon also publishes a free monthly guide to Chicago area apartments with extensive suburban listings.

## OTHER PLACES TO LOOK

Leases are stubborn, inflexible things and are rarely in sync with changes of career or heart. Because of this, people are constantly moving before their leases expire and are always looking for new renters to take their place (unless they want to forfeit their security deposit). Bulletin boards are a good place to look for sublets and short-term leases. Look for them in coffeehouses, laundromats, supermarkets, and anywhere there's a notice board.

If you need an inexpensive place for the summer months, you might check out the notice boards at a local college or university. Many college students leave during the summer and are desperate to find a renter who will take on the lease, sometimes for substantially less money.

Finally, you might consider calling some of the bigger neighborhood landlords and asking about vacancies. You can identify the larger landlords because they often have plaques with their names and phone numbers on the corners of their buildings.

## CHECKING IT OUT

You're on your way to the day's first rental appointment, you haven't had breakfast, the old college friend you're staying with is getting restless, your back is aching from a bad night's sleep, and twenty other people are waiting outside as you drive up — you panic, take a quick glance around, like what you see, and grab an application. Three months later you're wondering how you landed in such a dump.

To avoid this scenario, tour each apartment with a clear idea in your head of what you are looking for. Beyond these personal likes and dislikes, there are some specific things to check for as you look:

Is the apartment on the first floor? If so, does it have burglar bars? First-floor apartments are easy targets for burglary.

Are the appliances clean and in good working order? Test all of the stove's burners. Does the kitchen sink have one or two basins? Is there sufficient counter space?

Is heat included in your rent? If it is, you probably have steam heat with radiators. If the heat is extra, then you have either electric or gas heat. Neither is cheap, especially in winter. Gas bills can run more than $100 a month in a severe Chicago winter. Peoples Gas offers a plan where you can pay a regular monthly fee year-round to build an account and avoid getting socked with expensive winter heating bills. Commonwealth Edison should be able to give you an average bill for the unit.

Check the windows to make sure they open, close and lock. Are there operable storm windows? If not, are the windows thermal (with double panes of glass)? If none of the above, it's going to be cold near your windows in the winter. If you still like the apartment, you can cover the windows with plastic to insulate your apartment until spring, but this takes some work.

Do the windows, especially the bedroom windows open onto a busy street or alley? Alleys are especially notorious for late night car horns and loud early morning trash removal.

Are there enough closets? Are the closets big enough to accommodate your belongings?

Is there private storage space in a secure area?

Is there adequate water pressure for the shower, the sink and the toilet? Turn them on and check. Water pressure throughout Chicago is low; with older buildings the pipes can be clogged with deposits to the point where you might only get a trickle.

Flush all toilets and check for leaks or unusual noises.

Check the number of electrical outlets. In older buildings it is common to have one or two outlets per room. Are there enough outlets for all your plug-in appliances?

Are there laundry facilities in the building? Is there a laundromat within walking distance?

How close is the building to public transit and grocery stores?

If you're looking at a garden apartment, which is an elegant way of saying "basement apartment," check to see if there are any water stains along the walls? They're a sure sign of flooding.

Does it smell funny? They may have just sprayed the apartment for bugs; you should think twice before taking it. If it's a multi-unit building, there may be bugs in the other apartments just waiting to move in with you.

Is there a smoke detector as well as a carbon monoxide detector in the apartment? While landlords are only required by law to provide smoke detectors, carbon monoxide detectors are a good idea as well.

## STAKING A CLAIM

Once you have chosen an apartment, you will be asked to fill out an application. It is a good idea to have your references handy, both credit and personal: bank account numbers, credit cards, former landlord's name and phone number, and current and former employers.

Also, you should have your checkbook ready so you can make a deposit. Landlords are under no obligation to hold an apartment for you without a deposit. If the next prospective tenant likes the place and writes a deposit check, you are out of luck.

## MOVING

Most leases in Chicago start May 1 and October 1, which makes the last weekends in April and September a time of near chaos in certain neighborhoods. Since these are the busiest periods of the year, the truck-rental companies rent trucks in three four-hour shifts — from 8 a.m. to noon, noon to 4 p.m., and 4 p.m. to 8 p.m. Be sure to reserve a truck early (at least four weeks in advance) because they disappear fast and might not be available when you want to move.

## LEASES AND SECURITY DEPOSITS

The lease is a legally binding contract that outlines the landlord's responsibilities as well as your obligations as a tenant. It goes without saying that you should read your lease carefully before signing it.

The lease should state your name and address as well as the name and address of the landlord. It should state the first and last dates of your contracted occupancy, the monthly rent and where the rent is to be paid. Look for other riders that may be added to the contract concerning pets or waterbeds, for example. Remember that you don't have to sign the lease immediately. It's your right to examine the lease and return it at a mutually agreed-upon time.

Quite often you will be moving into your new apartment on the heels of the previous tenants, leaving no time for an inspection with your landlord. It's a good idea to make a note of any damage you find as you're moving in, photograph it and put it in writing to your landlord. Ask him or her to visit and verify the damage as soon as possible and attach it to the lease.

Landlords typically ask for one to two months' rent as security deposit to protect them from damages after a tenant moves out. After you move and if you leave your apartment in good condition, you are entitled to a refund of your security deposit within 45 days. If your landlord dawdles in returning your security deposit, you can file a claim in *pro se* court (where you don't need a lawyer to represent you) for up to double the amount of your deposit.

If you live in a building with 25 units or more, Illinois requires the landlord to pay interest on your security deposit.

Chicago's Residential Landlord and Tenant Ordinance, which was enacted in 1986 and amended in 1991, applies to tenants who live in all-rental units with written or oral leases. It does not apply to tenants living in owner-occupied buildings containing six units or less.

The ordinance spells out the contractual obligations landlord and tenant have toward each other. You can pick one up at the Chicago Department of Housing, 318 South Michigan Avenue, 312-747-1655, or you can buy a copy at the Office of the City Clerk, Room 107, 121 North LaSalle Street, 312-744-6861. Also, a tremendously useful book for those in the renting class: *The Chicago Tenant Handbook* by Ed Sachs.

Among their obligations, landlords must supply adequate heat from September 15 to June 1 (68° during the day and 63° at night), hot water, plumbing, security, extermination of pests, and perform general maintenance. If your landlord is not meeting these contractual requirements, your first recourse is to call and inform the landlord of the problem. If your request is not met within a reasonable time, you have the option of reducing your rent as outlined under the Tenants' Rights Ordinance. At this time, you may want to consult a lawyer or a tenant union.

Organizations that may be helpful in disputes with your landlord or provide more detailed information about your rights as a tenant include:

- **Chicago Department of Housing**, 318 South Michigan Avenue, 312-747-1655
- **Chicago Urban League**, 4750 South Michigan Avenue, 773-285-5800
- **Illinois Tenants Union**, 4616 North Drake Avenue, 773-478-1133
- **Lawyers Committee for Better Housing** (Edgewater and Rogers

Park), 407 South Dearborn Street, 312-347-7600
- **Legal Assistance Foundation of Chicago**, 312-341-1070
- **Metropolitan Tenants Organization**, 773-292-4988
- **Rogers Park Community Action Network (R.P.C.A.N.)**, 1545 West Morse, 773-973-7888

If you break your lease, your landlord can charge a subletting fee to cover his or her expenses in finding a new tenant for the apartment. It might be a good idea to find a new tenant on your own to save on these expenses.

## RENTER'S INSURANCE

You've moved into your new apartment, and the last boxes have been cleared away. Take a look around and ask yourself, "How much would it cost to start over if everything I see was destroyed by fire?" Probably more than you think. Imagine having to replace your clothing, television, stereo, music, furniture, computer, and other accumulations of a lifetime. The bill might be staggering.

With renter's insurance, you typically are protected against fire, hail, lightning, explosion, aircraft, smoke, vandalism, theft, building collapse, frozen plumbing, defective appliances and sudden electrical damage and more. Renters insurance also may cover personal liability as well as damage done (by you) to the property of others.

By now you should be convinced that renter's insurance is a good idea, especially because your belongings are not insured under your landlord's policy. The good news about renter's insurance is that it is not as expensive as you might believe. For $15,000 to $20,000 in coverage you probably will pay less than $300 a year, sometimes less than $250.

Before looking in the phone book or contacting your own insurance company, you might want to call the Illinois Department of Insurance at 312-814-2427. They keep track of all major companies' "complaint ratios" (number of complaints filed per year to dollars paid out each year). Tell them that you're interested in the ratios for renter's insurance, though ratios for other types of insurance are also available.

When shopping for renter's insurance, be sure to ask whether the insurance company pays as soon as the claim is filed and whether it pays cash value or replacement value. If you have a cash-value policy, you will only be paid what your five-year-old television is worth, not what it costs to replace it. Some big-ticket items such as home computers or furs and jewelry are insured only to a certain amount. Make sure you know what it is.

You can purchase renter's insurance through almost any insurance agency or company. Whether you get renter's insurance or not, it's a good idea to keep an inventory of all items of value and record their serial numbers.

## HOUSE, CONDO OR CO-OP HUNTING

Chicagoans love to own their own pads. In fact, by a substantial margin, the Windy City has more owner-occupied housing than any other U.S. metropolitan area. This fact is all the more remarkable given the sustained rise of real-estate prices in the last decade. Many of the city neighborhoods profiled in this book have led the charge. In the top ten list of neighborhoods whose home values increased the most in the 1990s are: Wicker Park (#1), Lincoln Park West (#3), Lincoln Park East (#4), DePaul (#5), Lakeview (#7), Bucktown (#9), and Wrigleyville (#10). Clearly, there is a revolution of sorts going on in the near North Side.

If you're in the market for a **condominium**, and you think you might want to rent out your unit in the future, keep in mind that condominium associations can restrict an owner's right to rent out his or her pad. The association even has the power to limit renting even if there is no specific ban on it in the association bylaws. As the *Sun-Times* reports, "renters have become such a problem for some associations that the associations are starting to declare them *persona non grata*." The message: like marriage, take the plunge only when you're ready to commit.

One thing to be aware of as you begin your search: Chicago is one of the few places in the country where you will find **co-cops** for sale. Co-ops, most popular in New York City, and only found in Chicago's pricier downtown and lakefront neighborhoods, are shares in a corporation that owns a residential building. Thus, as opposed to a condo which is outright ownership of a particular unit plus a share of the common area, buying a co-op entitles you to live in a percentage of the building, not in a particular unit. The corporation, not the individual owner, is king. If you are considering buying a co-op, realize that you will have get the approval of the co-op board which can ask very nosy questions in their effort to determine if your money is good enough.

If you're ready to jump on the home-buying bandwagon, you might want to consider the following strategies.

As with apartment hunting, perhaps the simplest way to look for a place to buy is to **drive around the neighborhood** you're interested in and look for "For Sale" signs — though, this may not work as well with units in large buildings since there may be no place to hang a sign outside.

The most obvious way to start your search is to **look in the newspapers**. Both the *Chicago Tribune* and the *Sun-Times* have extensive real estate sections. The *Tribune* also offers an online database of residential properties for sale at its web site: as well as a weekly "Your Place" section in Friday's paper.

Then there's the tried and true method: **work with a real estate agent or broker**. Ask around for a recommendation or look in the Yellow Pages under "Real Estate."

If you are computer savvy and want to narrow down the search on your own, many larger **real estate companies have web sites**. Here you can check out the available homes through photos, floorplans, community information, and organize your search along any lines. For starters, check out the following:

- **Baird & Warner** at *www.bairdwarner.com*
- **Koenig & Strey** at *www.koenig-strey.com*
- **The Prudential** at *www.pruhomes.com*

Or ask your real estate agent for the address of his or her company.
Two other realty sites worth visiting:

- **National Association of Realtors** at *www.realtor.com*
- **Realty Guide** at *www.xmission.com/~realtor1*

Another option for web-slingers is to check out internet sites which compile lists of **for-sale-by-owner homes**. Potentially, you can save a lot of money in broker costs by going this way, though the selection of properties to choose from is smaller. Here are three you might want to look into.

- **Abele Owners' Network** at *www.owners.com*
- **By Owner Online** at *www.by-owner-ol.com*
- **FiSBO Registry** at *www.fisbos.com*

Another good resource if you are looking in the northernmost Illinois counties is the **Multiple Listing Service of Northern Illinois**. They claim to list over half of the houses for sale in the northern counties. Try them at *www.cyberhouses.com* or *www.realtor.com/chicago*.

Good luck and happy hunting.

NOW THAT YOU'VE FOUND YOUR NEW APARTMENT, SIGNED your lease and are preparing to move in — what's next? Let's see, utilities and the telephone, voter registration, library card, driver's license, if you own a car — city sticker, and license plates . . .

## GAS UTILITIES

If you have an all-electric apartment, skip this section.

If you live in the city of Chicago and have gas heat or just a gas range for cooking, call **Peoples Gas**, 312-240-7000, to request service.

If you have only a gas range, your bill should be $15 - $20 a month.

If you have gas heat, you will be paying a considerably larger bill in winter than in summer. This may seem only logical, but the winter bills can be staggering, especially if you live in an older, draftier apartment. Peoples Gas does have a bill-averaging plan; the monthly bill depends on the size of your apartment. For example, if you have a one-bedroom apartment, Peoples Gas may charge you $50 a month year round. During the warmer months, your payments build up credit for the more expensive winter months. At the end of a year's service, you will pay the balance of what you owe or receive credit for your next year or next apartment if there are excess funds remaining. If you are leaving town, Peoples Gas will write you a check.

For those living in the North suburbs, including Deerfield, Glencoe, Highland Park, Northbrook, and Winetka, you will need to call **North Shore Gas Company**, a subsidiary of Peoples Gas, to request service. Their phone number is 708-336-9300.

Residents of Des Plaines, Evanston, Oak Park, Rosemont, Skokie, and Wilmette, among others, are served by **Nicor Gas Company**, previously known as Northern Illinois Gas Co. To request service call 800-942-6100.

## COMMONWEALTH EDISON

Commonwealth Edison, commonly referred to as Com Ed, is the electric company for the entire Chicagoland area. It is also the largest nuclear utility in the nation. (For those who like to worry, it should be noted that Illinois was recently home to four of the six nuclear plants on the Nuclear Regulatory Commission's national watch list.) For service, call 800-334-7661.

Commonwealth Edison has a light bulb service for its customers. For an extra fee each month, you are entitled to free light bulbs at certain bill-payment centers. Ask about this service when you sign up. To find the bill-payment and light bulb center nearest you, check the Yellow Pages under Electric Companies.

## WATER

Unless you're a homeowner, you won't be paying for your water. If you are paying, you may notice that your bill is the same every quarter. Through some regulatory fluke, residential rates are determined by building size and water usage is not metered. Whether you're paying for it or not, the water here may surprise you, especially if you're moving from an area where the water source is less compromised. In Chicago tap water comes from Lake Michigan, and while it ends up perfectly safe to drink (after extensive filtering and treatment), the taste of chlorine and residual pollutants can take some getting used to.

Bottled water is an option but over time it's more expensive than even the priciest filters. Water filter pitchers and faucet attachments are available at most hardware and department stores. These will take out the most offensive element — the chlorine taste — but they have only a modest impact on other pollutants. If you're really concerned, you can buy more expensive filters which attach directly to the water line.

It should be stressed that Chicago water meets or exceeds both the EPA's and the Illinois Pollution Control Board's standards for water purity. And, believe it or not, Chicago water is better than much of the groundwater in the area; to wit, 40 percent of the water that is pumped out of the lake is sold to neighboring suburbs.

## TELEPHONE SERVICE

Whether you are calling across town or around the world, in Chicago your connection still starts with that not so little baby bell, **Ameritech**. To order service, call toll-free, 800-244-4444. Most apartments in Chicago have phone jacks; just plug in your telephone, and Ameritech will switch you on. (You must supply your own phone.) There is a connection fee of $55 for home customers. If your apartment does not have phone jacks, ask your landlord to put them in. If your landlord doesn't, Ameritech charges $35 for a visit and $17.50 for each 15 minutes its representative is working in your apartment.

Ameritech offers various options such as Call Waiting, Three-Way Calling, Speed Calling, Distinctive Ringing, Call Forwarding and Voice Mail. These options will be explained to you by your service representative when you establish service, and they are detailed in the front of the White Pages phone book. At that time you also will be asked to name your preferred long-distance carrier. The major league long distance carriers are: **AT&T** (800-244-4444), **MCI/Worldcom** (800-888-8000) or **US Sprint** (800-877-7746).

When you leave your apartment, call 800-244-4444 to disconnect service and re-establish it at your new place. There is no charge to disconnect service.

With the ever increasing number of cell phones, pagers, phone and fax lines, Chicago, like the rest of the country, is grappling with area code issues. The city was recently divided into two area codes (the old 312 and the new 773) and this created some confusion for natives and newcomers alike. The borders of the 312 (central Chicago) area code are North Avenue, Western Avenue, and 35th Street. If you live south, east, and north of these streets you're a 312. If you don't, you're a 773. If only life were so simple. The truth is the border between the two zones is not neat. If you live near the border, you could be in either one. If you have a Chicago number and you're not sure as to the area code, open to the beginning of the White Pages. By looking at the first three digits of the phone number (the prefix) and checking it against the list of 773 prefixes, you can determine the area code. If you live in the suburbs, you could have one of five different area codes — 847, 815, 630, 708 or 815 — depending on where you live.

Just as the dust is settling on this latest area code split, Ameritech is proposing additional area codes, much to the dismay and outrage of Chicago area residents and business owners. Only time will tell whether more splits may be averted by going instead to the once dreaded "overlay" system. Such a system would require all callers to dial eleven digits, whether calling their next door neighbor or a neighboring suburb. The overlay system makes the geographical location of a caller a non-issue and simply assigns everyone, regardless of where they work or live, an eleven digit number.

Finally, if you feel frustrated with Ameritech, know that you're not alone. Contact the Illinois Commerce Commission (312-814-2887) or your Congressman with your complaint and join the Citizen's Utility Board (800-669-5556) in their effort to open and improve local telephone service.

## CELLULAR PHONE AND PAGING SERVICES

Following are some of the city's major cellular service providers. Check the Yellow Pages for a provider in your neighborhood.

- **AT&T Wireless Service**, 800-IMAGINE
- **Ameritech Cellular**, 800-MOBILE-1
- **CellularONE**, 800-CELL-ONE
- **Nextel**, 800-NEXTEL9
- **NovaCellular** (MCI), 800-571-NOVA
- **PrimeCo**, 800-801-2100

Here are some well-known pager suppliers. Check the Yellow Pages under "Paging" for more providers.

- **Apple Beeper**, 312-467-4112
- **Becker Beeper**, 800-GO-BECKER
- **MCI paging**, 800-695-4555
- **MobileComm**, 800-437-2337
- **PAGENET**, 312-621-4500

## UTILITY COMPLAINTS

If you have problems with any utility company (gas, electric, water, phone, cable TV) and they don't handle it to your satisfaction, don't hesitate to call the **Consumer Affairs Division of the Illinois Commerce Commission** at 312-814-2887. They are required to take your complaint; how helpful they can be is another matter.

Another group which looks out for consumer's interests is the **Citizens Utility Board** (CUB), 208 S. LaSalle, Suite 1760, Chicago, IL 60604, 800-669-5556. CUB is a consumer watchdog organization, constantly on the alert for excessive utility rate hikes. Over the years, they have successfully lobbied for lower rate increases, and even rate reductions and refunds.

# DRIVER'S LICENSES, AUTOMOBILE REGISTRATION, AND ILLINOIS STATE I.D.'S

If you own a car and live in Illinois, you must have an Illinois driver's license and Illinois license plates. If you live in Chicago, your vehicle must have a Chicago City Sticker. And what exactly is a City Sticker? It's one of those nasty, gummy things you attach to the inside of your windshield. Think of it as a yearly usage fee for the "privilege" of parking on city streets.

Illinois driver's licenses also are obtained through the Illinois Secretary of State. You'll need your old driver's license, your social security card, and proof of your new address (a utility bill or voters registration card will do). You will be asked to take a written test based on Illinois Rules of the Road and an eye test. The fee for an Illinois driver's license is just $10.

The State of Illinois requires all gasoline-powered cars and light trucks (diesel-powered vehicles are excepted) to undergo a biannual (once every two years) auto emissions test starting in the third year of the car's life. Drivers will receive notification in the mail. If you fail to report, you'll lose your driver's license eventually.

Illinois license plates can be purchased at any office of the Illinois Secretary of State or at neighborhood currency exchanges. The price of the license plates depends on your vehicle. Vanity plates are extra.

There are four **Illinois Secretary of State** offices in Chicago:

- State of Illinois Building, 100 West Randolph Street, 312-793-1010
- North, 5401 North Elston Avenue, 773-794-5821
- South, 9901 South King Drive, 773-995-2615
- West, 5301 West Lexington Street, 773-854-4808

For those moving to Illinois with a leased vehicle, there's a bit more work involved to register it with the state. Bring your car's old lease and registration information to the Secretary of State's office (see above), where you will not only pay for normal registration, but will also file an RUT25 form for leased car tax. The tax on a leased vehicle is figured according to the following formula: the price on your lease agreement states the car's worth/value, for each month you've had the car, the Illinois Dept. of Revenue figures a two percent depreciation bringing it down to its current estimated value. They will then tax the car at seven percent (in Chicago) of that depreciated value. However, if you have an affidavit from your leasing company that reports how much you have already paid them in taxes, the Illinois Dept. of Revenue will subtract that amount from your figured tax. Be aware, you have 30 days, from the time the car enters Illinois, to file this RUT25 form to avoid a two percent extra late filing charge and a 15 percent extra late payment charge, equaling an additional 17 percent tacked on to the figured leased vehicle tax. Call the **Illinois Department of Revenue** at 800-732-8866 with any questions.

If you don't drive but need a photo identification, you can get an Illinois identification card, which is as good as a driver's license when proof of identity is required. You can get the Illinois ID through the Illinois Secretary of State.

City stickers can be purchased for $60 at the **City Clerk's Office** in Room 107 of City Hall, 121 North LaSalle Street, 312-744-6861, or at neighborhood currency exchanges, where you'll have to pay a $3 to $5 service charge. They are valid from July 1st to June 30th of the next year. If you buy your sticker more than 30 days after the renewal date, an additional $30 fee will be assessed. The ticket price for not having a sticker is $60, so don't gamble that they won't find you — they will. The city has access to the Illinois Secretary of State's records so it's easy for a meter reader to enter a plate number on a computer and see if you should have a sticker.

Should you be so unfortunate as to receive a ticket for a moving violation or illegal parking in Chicago, **Traffic Court** is at 321 North LaSalle Street, 312-822-3604. If you receive a ticket for a moving violation, you must report on the day stated on your ticket to enter a plea and then you will be assigned a court date. Be aware that in Illinois you must post bond when you receive a moving violation citation. If you do not have a spare $75 in cash or a bail bond card (available through many automobile clubs such as AAA or Allstate) the officer will take your license until you post bond or pay your fine. This can be a huge inconvenience.

## PARKING

Parking ticket fines start at $15 and rise to $100 depending on the offense. Your fine will be marked on the ticket. If you want to fight the parking ticket, mail back the envelope after marking an "X" in the box requesting a hearing. The city will send a card telling you when to go for your hearing. Or you can contest the ticket by mail, writing your reasons why you didn't deserve the ticket. The city will respond, informing you whether or not you will have to pay the ticket. For more information about a specific parking violation call the city's **Office of Parking Ticket Inquiries** at 312-744-7275. Good luck.

Parking in Chicago varies depending upon location. Permit parking is the rage in many popular neighborhoods in order to save on-street parking places for residents. Lincoln Park, DePaul/Lincoln Park West and Wrigleyville/Lakeview are particularly hard to park in without a permit and tow trucks cruise through these areas with cruel regularity. If you're not sure whether your neighborhood requires a parking permit, you can call your ward office or, easier still, walk down the block and look for parking regulation signs. You can't miss them. If you do live in a permit zone, once you get your annual permit parking sticker, purchase (they're cheap) one-day guest parking permits for visitors.

If you are towed, call the **Police Department Auto Pound**, 312-747-5513, to find out where your vehicle was taken. To retrieve your wheels, you must pay a $105 towing fee plus a $10 per day holding fee. You must pay cash or use VISA or MasterCard; personal checks are not allowed.

It should be noted that while parking tickets were once easily ignored, these days the city is serious, very serious, about collecting fines. Five unpaid tickets can result in your car being "booted," an ignominious not to mention inconvenient occurence.

Be aware, Illinois requires a license plate on both the front end and back end of your car. Failure to comply can result in a $25 fine. A broken windshield will get you the same. Both fines can be issued at the same time your expired parking meter citation is being written.

## STOLEN CARS

If it turns out your car has been stolen, not towed, the police will need your license and city sticker numbers, the car's year, make, model and color as well as the vehicle identification number. You also should mark your sound system, radar detector, car phone, and other accessories with your driver's license number. You can borrow an engraving pen through your local police district's Operation Identification program.

## VOTER REGISTRATION

The old Chicago election day slogan, "Vote early and often," is a reminder of days gone by when the city played fast and loose with election results. Today, Chicago elections are honest.

To register to vote in Chicago, go to City Hall offices of the **Board**

of Election Commissioners, 121 North LaSalle Street, 312-269-7960.
You need two pieces of identification; one must have your current
address. This is also the office for requesting an absentee ballot or
changing your voter's registration.

Close to election time, voter registration drives are held throughout
the city. In many cases, you will be able to register with a volunteer in
less than five minutes.

Political campaigns make for exciting times in Chicago. Here are
some places for those who want to take a more active role:

- **Democratic Party of Cook County**, 30 North LaSalle Street, Suite
  2432, 312-263-0575
- **Republican Party of Cook County**, 16 North Wabash Avenue, 312-
  977-1467
- **Independent Voters of Illinois**, 201 North Wells Street, 312-236-5705
- **League of Women Voters**, 332 South Michigan Avenue, Suite 1142,
  312-939-5935

## LIBRARIES

You can apply for a Chicago Public Library card at any Chicago Public
Library. It's simple and fast. Best of all, library cards are free.

In addition to the **Harold Washington Public Library**, the city's
jewel of a central library (400 South State Street, 312-747-4300; open
Monday 9 a.m.-7 p.m., Tuesdays and Thursdays 11 a.m.-7 p.m.,
Wednesday, Friday and Saturday 9 a.m.-5 p.m., Sunday 1 p.m.-5 p.m.)
and the Chicago Public Library's neighborhood branches throughout
the city (they're listed at the end of each neighborhood section), there
are university and independent libraries that are available to Chicagoans.
Many are closed on Sunday and/or Monday, so call first.

- **Art Institute of Chicago Library**, Michigan Avenue at Adams Street,
  312-443-3666
- **Chicago Historical Society Library**, 1601 North Clark Street, 312-
  642-4600
- **DePaul University Libraries:** Lincoln Park, 2350 North Kenmore
  Avenue, 773-325-7862; Loop Campus, 1 East Jackson Drive, 312-
  362-8433; Law Library, 25 East Jackson Drive, 312-362-8121
- **Loyola University Library**, 6525 North Sheridan Road, 773-508-2631
- **Newberry Library**, 60 West Walton Street, 312-943-9090

- **Northwestern University Library,** 1935 Sheridan, Evanston, 847-491-7658
- **University of Chicago Regenstein Library,** 1100 East 57th Street, 773-702-7874
- **University of Illinois-Chicago,** 801 South Morgan Street, 312-996-2726

## NEWSPAPERS AND MAGAZINES

Whether your interest is in theater, where the best poetry readings take place or the trendiest restaurants, there is probably a local (and often free) publication to suit you. And since Chicago is one of the few remaining cities with competing daily newspapers, the *Chicago Sun-Times* and the *Chicago Tribune*, news coverage is sharp, ground-breaking (the local television news stations regularly pick up stories from the two dailies) and thorough. For more in-depth regional news and business, *Crain's Chicago Business* is regarded as one of the best weeklies in the country. Since all three publications are news-heavy (the *Sun-Times* focus is on local news; the *Tribune* covers more national and international news), the alternative papers such as the *Reader* and *New City* are feature-driven, as is the monthly *Chicago Magazine*. There are also various student and independent magazines available in area coffeehouses and record stores, although it is best to stick with the *Reader* or *New City* for dependable movie, club, or theater listings. Two local papers which cover news and events with an emphasis on Chicago's African-American community are *N'DIGO* and the *Chicago Daily Defender*. *N'DIGO* is a free weekly paper with listings, reviews, editorials, and feature articles. The *Chicago Daily Defender* covers local and national news.

- *Chicago Daily Defender,* 2400 South Michigan Avenue, 60616. 312-225-2400
- *Chicago Magazine,* 500 North Dearborn Street, 60610. 312-222-8999 or 800-999-0879
- *Chicago Reader* (free in shops, restaurants, clubs all over the North Side and selected South Side areas and suburbs), 11 East Illinois Street, 60611, 312-828-0350.
- *Chicago Sun-Times,* 401 North Wabash Avenue, 60611, 312-321-3000 or 800-945-5000
- *Chicago Tribune,* 435 North Michigan Avenue, 60611, 312-222-3232 or 800-TRIBUNE; electronic edition (Chicago Tribune Online)

800-922-0808; talk support 800-827-6568.
- *Crain's Chicago Business,* 740 North Rush Street, 60611, 312-649-5200, also available through Chicago Online (see number above).
- *N'DIGO* (free in shops, restaurants, all over Chicago), 401 North Wabash Avenue, Suite 534, 60611, 312-822-0202.
- *New City* (free in shops, restaurants and clubs inside Chicago), 770 North Halsted Street, Suite 208, 60622, 312-243-8786.

## NATIONAL ONLINE SERVICES

- **America Online,** 800-827-6364
- **AT&T,** 800-222-0300
- **Microsoft Network,** 800-426-9400
- **Netcom,** 800-638-2661
- **Prodigy,** 800-776-3449
- **Voyager,** 888-747-4NET
- **Whole Earth Network,** 415-281-6500

## TELEVISION STATIONS

Provided you have a good antenna and you don't live in a basement or in a highrise, you should be able to receive the following network and local independent stations without cable service:

Channel 2 WBBM/CBS
Channel 5 WMAQ/NBC
Channel 7 WLS/ABC
Channel 9 WGN (independent)
Channel 11 WTTW/Public Broadcasting System
Channel 20 WYCC (Public Broadcasting System affiliated with Chicago City Colleges)
Channel 26 WCIU (independent)
Channel 32 WFLD/Fox
Channel 44 WSNS (independent)
Channel 50 WPWR (independent)
Channel 66 WGBO (independent)

Daily program listings are printed in both the *Chicago Sun-Times* and the *Chicago Tribune* and their weekly TV magazines, as well as in *TV Guide.*

# CABLE TELEVISION

Chicago is divided into five areas for cable service from two cable television companies: Chicago Cable TV (a TCI company), 773-434-6976 and Prime Cable of Chicago, 773-736-1800. Each company offers basic cable service with the premium channels available for an extra fee; there are slight differences in channels and programming.

To find out which cable area you are in, call the **City of Chicago Cable Communications - Administration, Information and Complaints**, 312-744-4052.

# RADIO STATIONS

If you can't make it through the day without morning talk radio, National Public Radio or Rush Limbaugh, here are Chicago's radio stations along with the type of music or talk they broadcast:

**FM Dial**
88.1 WCRX, Dance music
89.3 WNUR Northwestern University Radio
90.1 WMBI Christian
91.5 WBEZ Public Radio by day (NPR); jazz at night
92.7 WCBR Adult rock
93.1 WXRT Album-oriented-rock, folk, blues and reggae
93.9 WLIT Adult contemporary
94.7 WXCD Classic rock, new format
95.5 WNUA Jazz and new age
96.3 WBBM Top 40 rock
97.1 WNIB Classical
97.9 WLUP Adult rock
98.7 WFMT Classical
99.5 WUSN Country
100.3 WPNT Adult contemporary
101.1 WKQX Top 40/alternative rock
101.9 WTMX Oldies (60s, 70s, 80s)
102.7 WVAZ Black contemporary
103.5 WRCX Rock
104.3 WJMK Oldies (50s, 60s, early 70s)
105.1 WOJO Spanish contemporary
105.9 WCKG Classic rock, talk.

106.7 WYLL Christian
107.5 WGCI Black contemporary
107.9 WYSY All '70's

**AM Dial**
560 WIND Spanish contemporary
670 WMAQ News, White Sox, Bulls games
720 WGN Talk radio, Cubs games
780 WBBM News
890 WLS Talk radio
930 WAUR Oldies
1000 WMVP Talk radio and sports (including the Bulls)
1110 WMBI Christian
1160 WJJD Oldies
1240 WEDC Foreign language variety
1390 WGCI Oldies
1570 WBEE Jazz, blues and gospel

## PETS

If you're going to keep a dog in Chicago, he or she will need a rabies vaccination and you will need a dog license. The former are available at any
vet; they will also give you a vaccination tag to put on your dog's collar.
Dog licenses are available at the **City Clerk's Office**, 121 North La Salle
Street, 312-744-6875, but you will need proof of a rabies vaccination to
get one. Dog licenses cost $5 ($2 for seniors), are valid for one year, and
expire on April 30th. It's strongly recommended that you make sure your
dog wears his or her tags at all times, otherwise if Muffy gets lost you may
never see her again. Chicago also has a leash law and a waste removal
(scoop the poop) law so bring a bag or some newspaper when you walk
your four-legged friend For violating any of the above ordinances you can
be fined $200.

During the summer (Memorial day to Labor day) from 9 a.m. to 9
p.m., dogs are not allowed on the beaches. However, you will find a
multitude of frolicking slap-happy, water loving dogs on the beach in
the early mornings. During the day, check out Belmont Harbor just
north of Belmont Avenue; there's a small spit of beach there which, on
the weekends, is more dog than beach. And, just across the harbor, near
the Recreation Drive exit off of Lake Shore Drive, there's another dog
get-together spot called "Bark Park." If you don't live near the lake and

want companionship for your pup, just wake up early and walk on over to the nearest neighborhood park. All over the city, parks are transformed into early morning doggie play groups. Just remember to pick up the poop! Don't panic if you don't have the time to walk your dog every day, there are plenty of dog-walking services. Just look in the Yellow Pages under "Pet Exercising Services."

As for cats, they don't need licenses, but they must get a rabies vaccination. If you lose your cat or dog, first contact your local police district. Then make sure you talk to neighbors, postal carriers or sanitation workers for leads. Also check out the Lost/Found ads in your local newspaper and put up signs in the neighborhood. In Chicago call the following services to see if someone found your pet:

- **Animal Control Center**, 312-744-5000
- **Animal Welfare Society**, 312-667-0088
- **The Anti-Cruelty Society**, 312-644-8338
- **Tree House (cats only)**, 312-784-5488

If you want a dog or cat, and also want to perform a good deed, you can adopt a pet at the **City of Chicago's Commission on Animal Care and Control**, 2741 South Western Avenue, 312-744-5000. A dog, spayed or neutered, with license and all necessary shots, will cost you $57. A cat will set you back $50. The Anti-Cruelty Society, 510 North LaSalle Street, 312-667-0088, also offers an adoption service for abandoned pets. The fee is a flat $50 for cats or dogs and includes the necessary shots, a free collar, an ID chip, but not spay or neutering (though these services are available for an additional fee). Adoption is more than just a cheap way to get a pet (all these services together would be two or three times as much at a vet), it's a way to save its life. Whatever you do, make sure you that your dog or cat is spayed or neutered.

## MAIL DELIVERY

Newcomers are sometimes unaware of Chicago's terrible reputation when it comes to delivering mail. In the past, thousands of undelivered pieces of mail were discovered in the apartments and houses of carriers not to mention tossed in garbage dumpsters. While reform has been glacial, a federal task force resulted in important management changes, and as a result, service has improved (though cynics point out it could hardly have gotten worse). If you experience a problem with your postal service, we suggest you contact the **USPS Office of Consumer Affairs,** 312-983-8400, at the new main post office downtown at 433 West Harrison. If that doesn't work, contact your Congress-person; they may be able to help.

## PASSPORTS

You can apply for a passport at the U.S. State Department office in the Federal Building, 230 South Dearborn Street, Room 380. You can hear a full explanation of the application process by calling 312-353-7155. Figure on three to four weeks for your application to be processed. If you're in a hurry, you can pay an extra $30 for expedited service which should give you your passport in three business days.

If you are applying for the first time or if it has been more than 12 years since you last received a passport or if your passport has been lost or stolen, you must submit five items in application: 1) proof of U.S. citizenship; 2) two identical photos taken within the last six months; 3) evidence of identity; 4) $65 for the application fee; and 5) a completed passport application form, DSP-11.

Passports are valid for 10 years.

## RECYCLING

Chicago's Blue Bag recycling program began in 1995. The concept is quite simple. Recyclables are divided into three categories: clean containers (plastic, aluminum, steel, or glass); clean wastepaper (newspapers, magazines, junk mail, phone books, paper); and yard waste. Recyclables from each category are put into three separate blue garbage bags. When the bags are full they are put in your city-supplied trash can (or landlord-supplied dumpster). Blue bags are available at most grocery stores and hardware stores in different sizes. Call the **Blue Bag Hotline** at 312-BLUE BAG if you have any questions.

From the beginning, the Blue Bag program was criticized by environmentalists for being ineffective, labor intensive, and voluntary. In many other cities the sorting of recyclables is more thorough but the citizens do it themselves and it is picked up by separate recycling trucks. By combining recyclable collection with the regular weekly garbage pickup, Chicago saved the expense of buying new trucks. But it did have to build four huge processing plants where all the city's garbage is emptied onto conveyor belts and sorted through. The city is hoping that the initial

drawbacks of the program — low participation rates and high labor costs-
- will be offset in the future by higher participation rates, once people
learn how easy it is to recycle. As it is, the program has been judged a
success with greater participation than expected.

For those who still want to sort the old-fashioned way (glass, metal,
paper and plastics) the **Resource Center** runs two independent recycling centers, including one in Lincoln Park in the parking lot of the 7-
Eleven on the northwest corner of Sheffield, Wrightwood and Lincoln
Avenues. They can also give you information on other recycle/reuse programs throughout the city. Call them at 773-821-1351.

**Uptown Recycling**, 773-769-4488, also runs an independent
drop-off center at 4753 North Broadway.

## WEATHER

Like much of the midwest, Chicago enjoys four distinct seasons, and
though the city has an (undeserved, we think) reputation for harsh winters, they are nothing like the winters in snowy Buffalo or arctic
Minneapolis-St. Paul. In fact, the sweltering summers in Chicago can be
much more unpleasant, not to mention dangerous, with high tempera-
tures and humid conditions.

Strong winds along the lakeshore keep the areas close to the lake
slightly cooler in the summer and warmer and more humid in the winter. Winter snowstorms, when they come, usually hit between
December and April.

The party line on winter dress for downtown commuters is "heavy
and waterproof." If you are moving to Chicago from a warmer part of
the country you may want to purchase boots, gloves and a hat,
although some rugged individuals scoff at this approach and simply run
from their house to the train or their car to their office . . . The spring and
summer months are the time to get winterwear bargains; try Burlington
Coat Factory (Harlem-Foster Plaza, 7340 West Foster Avenue, 773-763-
6006) for reasonable prices on outerwear.

## SAFETY & CRIME

Chicago, like all big American cities, has its share of crime, however, like
all big American cities, it has seen its crime rate drop in the past decade
(since 1991, violent crime in Chicago is down 28% ). That said, there are
a few common sense things that a newcomer to the Windy City, espe-

cially a newcomer to urban life, should keep in mind:

- Trust your intuition. If something doesn't feel right, go with it. You're not being paranoid, you're feeling healthy survival instincts.
- When outside, keep your eyes and ears open. Always remaining alert and aware of your surroundings is key to personal safety.
- Don't let a stranger get in your car and don't get in a car with a stranger. Studies show that once you are in a vehicle with a would-be criminal, your chances of survival go way down.
- Don't move into a neighborhood that you are not comfortable with. Before you take an apartment, you should walk around the neighborhood to see what the area is like.
- Make sure your apartment or home is safe from potential intruders. That means, for example, that if you are on a ground floor or in a garden apartment, you should probably have sturdy bars on your windows. Err on the side of caution when assessing your risk.
- On the "L," try to sit in a car with other people.
- Resist the temptation to travel alone or at night through a neighborhood that you are uncertain or afraid of. It's better to be safe than sorry.
- If something does happen to you, whether you are in your home or car or on the street, remember that most incidences of crime do not result in loss of life. However, if you feel your life may be in danger, run, scream, fight, whatever it takes, to save your life. In life-threatening situations, being passive may not be the best response.
- Report crime. Whether it's happening to you or not, call 911 when you know of any crime in progress. If we don't work together, life will be harder for all and we will return to the dark days of relentless crime rate increases. Note, for non-emergency police questions, call 312-744-4000; they can tell you the location of your nearest District or Area police headquarters.

## SERVICES FOR THE DISABLED

The **Mayor's Office for People with Disabilities** (MOPD), 312-744-6673 or 312-744-7833 TTY, is an excellent resource, offering services and programs to Chicagoans with disabilities. MOPD provides case management services, employment services, skills training, information on how to find accessible housing, emergency home-delivered meals, recreation programs, and a host of other services for the disabled. They even have a pamphlet for business owners which details the tax-incentives available for making facilities accessible to people with disabilities. For a complete list of services, call, or write them at City Hall, 121 North LaSalle Street, Room 1104, 60602.

For the hearing and visually impaired, the organization called **Contact Chicago**, 4750 North Sheridan Road, #102, 773-728-0780; TTY 773-728-7724, provides anonymous/confidential telephone listening and a helpline as well as crisis intervention and peer counseling.

**Chicago Lighthouse**, 1850 West Roosevelt Road, 312-666-1331, TTY 312-666-8874, as well as the **Guild for the Blind**, 180 North Michigan Avenue #1700, 312-236-8569, provides employment and independent living services for the blind and visually impaired. The **Illinois Regional Library for the Blind**, 1055 West Roosevelt Road, 312-746-9210, offers books in braille and recorded books on cassette.

Check the Yellow pages under "Disabled Persons" for more resources.

## GAY & LESBIAN LIFE

Chicago *is* a good place to live if you're gay or lesbian. The city, like all of Cook County, has anti-bias statutes in place to protect gays and lesbians from housing and workplace discrimination. Progressive suburb Oak Park was the first municipality in Illinois to offer domestic partner benefits to city employees (Chicago followed suit in 1996). Recently, Chicagoans elected the first openly gay Illinois state representative. Most important, the Windy City seems to have finally taken to heart the slogan "We're here, we're queer, get used to it."

If you're looking for gay nightlife, the answer is easy. While it may not have the reputation of New York's Greenwich Village or San Francisco's Castro, Boystown in Wrigleyville/Lakeview is as out and proud as either. The neighborhood, which is centered on Halsted Street between Belmont Avenue and Irving Park Road, is the backbone of gay Chicago. But the boys don't have all the fun. Andersonville, which is located two miles to the north along Clark Street, is becoming a favorite hangout for the city's lesbian community. Which isn't to say that you should live in either neighborhood if you're gay, or that everyone in them is gay. Chicago is big and open-minded enough that gays and lesbians are welcome anywhere.

To find out what's going on in the gay or lesbian community, you'll want to pick up a copy of the *Windy City Times* (Sentury Publications,

325 West Huron Street, 312-397-0025) or *Outlines* (Lambda Publications, 1115 West Belmont Avenue, 773-871-7610). Both free weeklies (though Outlines costs $2 in the suburbs) are available at coffeehouses, bookstores, and music stores throughout the North Side. For more indepth information about gay and lesbian Chicago, check out *Gay USA* by George Hobica or *Gay USA: Where the Babes Go!* by Lori Hobkirk. Both guides contain extensive listings of gay-owned (or gay-friendly) restaurants, bars, and stores throughout the city.

Also, there's a new branch of the public library devoted exclusively to gay and lesbian publications and concerns: the **Gerber/Hart Library** at 3352 North Paulina, 773-883-3003. They offer discussion groups, photography displays, a visiting author series and "a free cup of coffee." Closed Mondays and Tuesdays.

Last but not least, plan to attend the **Gay & Lesbian Pride Parade** which takes place at the end of June and starts at the corner of Halsted and Belmont (where else?). Everyone dresses just as they want — up, down, in drag, in leather, chests bared, in costume — and a great time is had by all.

# MONEY MATTERS

T O EASE YOUR FINANCIAL TRANSITION TO YOUR NEW CITY, here is some information about personal savings and checking accounts, credit cards and taxes.

## BANKING

One of the first things you will have to do after moving to Chicago is open a bank account. You will need to decide whether to bank near your place of employment or in your neighborhood (although some of the mega-banks are large enough to offer both). Banking near your job means you can dash out during lunch or right after work to take care of any transactions; banks located downtown tend to be larger financial institutions with a wider range of services than neighborhood banks. On the other hand, neighborhood banks provide more personal service within walking distance of your home. If you find the range and quality of banking services, e.g., favorable interest rates and minimum account requirements, more important than location, shop around. Your neighborhood may have a branch of one of the big downtown banks, allowing you to combine the best of both worlds.

Given banking deregulation and the industry upheavals that followed, traditional distinctions between commercial banks, savings banks and brokerage houses have become blurred. There are no set rules anymore. Banks are trying to lure customers by offering special windows for affluent customers and business clients or fee-free regular checking accounts. (But read that fine print: some banks may require only a $500 minimum balance, others as much as $1,500; and all of them are trying to slip in fees for things you never thought a bank would charge for. Today, more than ever, it pays to read the fine print.)

What else? Think about what is important to you . . . number of automatic teller machines (ATMs) in the bank's system and their locations, debit cards, online banking, traveler's checks, no or low fees . . . you decide.

Note: if you are a member of a credit union, this may be your best banking option. Credit unions generally offer affordable banking/financial service packages to their members. Look into whether your place of work or professional organization offers a credit union membership

## CHECKING ACCOUNTS

Obtain an application at the bank of your choice and fill it out — two references are often required, usually the name of your current or previous bank and that of your employer — together with two signed pieces of identification: a driver's license, credit card, draft card, or student ID with photo are all acceptable. It's also a good idea to bring checks along from your previous checking account. If your checking account was in good standing at your previous institution the new bank will often begin your new checks at a higher number. Some banks will require a minimum start-up deposit, some don't. Your account can be opened immediately, but checks and deposit slips won't be issued until your signature is verified. Some firms arrange for employees to open accounts at their own banks, which facilitates the process and may be fee-free; check with your benefits officer.

The best advice when choosing a bank is to shop around and compare services and fees. Some banks allow you 15 checks per month before they begin charging a per check fee, some allow unlimited checking and charge only a monthly service fee. "Regular" or non-interest-earning personal checking accounts that eliminate service charges as long as a minimum daily balance is maintained are standard today. But beware, banks charge anywhere from $9 to $15 if the account falls below the minimum daily balance. Also, find out if they charge you to use an ATM or (believe it or not) to use a teller; different banks have different fee policies. Another way to obtain fee-free checking is to link a money market, certificate of deposit or savings account kept in the same bank to your checking account. Service charges are added for any month when the balance drops below the specified minimum. Similar charges are levied on interest-earning "NOW" checking accounts if they fall below required minimum balances.

The latest trend banks are using to lure prospective customers is "free" checking. With such an account you can generally expect no monthly fees, no minimum balance and unlimited use of your checking account. Of course, there is no truly free lunch, as the saying goes, and these accounts usually do not earn interest.

## SAVINGS ACCOUNTS

Follow the preceding checking account instructions to apply for a "statement" savings account that provides monthly statements of all transactions and can be linked to your checking account. Most banks require an average minimum balance. If you fail to meet the requirement, you'll have to pay a service charge.

Once you have established good banking and credit relationships, you can apply for a mortgage, an auto, personal or education loan and credit cards. Your bank will probably issue you a cash card to access available funds in your checking and savings account. You can also get a debit card, which has the VISA or MasterCard logo on it and can be used anywhere a credit card is used. The difference is that it withdraws the funds directly from your checking account; make sure you keep a copy of all your receipts to help balance your checkbook. Cash cards (or ATM cards) can be used at any ATM (often called "Cash Stations" in Chicago), but you will probably be charged a fee if you use a machine that does not belong to your bank. A word of caution, a debit card generally will not be accepted for hotel or car reservations.

## CREDIT CARDS

If you haven't been inundated with "pre-approved" credit card applications, don't feel bad. You can find credit card applications in most stores — or call to request one.

**American Express** has two locations in the Loop and on North Michigan Avenue for your convenience. They are: 122 South Michigan Avenue, 312-435-2595; 625 North Michigan Avenue, 312-435-2570. Each office provides the full range of American Express services from the purchase of Traveler's Cheques to exchanging money to travel assistance. If your American Express Card has been lost or stolen, call Cardmember Services, 800-528-4800. If you need a refund for lost or stolen Traveler's Cheques, call 800-221-7282.

An American Express branch corporate office is located at 300 South Riverside Plaza, 9th floor south, 466-5400. You can make American Express payments here.

**Diner's Club Card** issues one card that costs $80 per year and requires proof of an annual income of at least $25,000. You can apply for the Diner's Club Card over the phone by calling 800-962-7070. If your Diner's Club Card has been lost or stolen, call Customer Service toll-free, 800-234-6377.

**Discover Cards** are issued by Morgan Stanley Dean Witter Discover. You can apply for one by calling 800-347-2683. There is no annual fee and the income required is a modest $15,000. Discover also issues a Private Issue Card, which carries an $18 annual fee and requires higher income. With both cards, you get cash back at the end of each anniversary year depending on how much you charged on the card. Payments on Discover Cards can still be made at Sears Roebuck & Co.

**VISA** and **MasterCard** can be obtained from various sources, usually banks, but everyone seems to issue these cards nowadays. If you keep a balance on your card, you will probably want one with a low interest rate, if you are compulsive about debt and pay off the balance every month, then you will most likely want the one with a low (or no) annual fee. Shop around for the best deal for you.

Although virtually all the major Chicago area department stores accept American Express and/or VISA and MasterCard, many issue their own credit cards (applications are available at customer service). Store charge accounts offer advantages over the major credit cards: advance notice of sales, mail or phone orders, no annual fee, and in some cases, spreading payments over a period of time for an added finance charge.

## TAXES

Federal income tax forms may be obtained in the lobby of the Federal Building, 230 South Dearborn Street, 17th floor or at some local post offices. Call 800-829-3676 or 312-435-1040 to obtain literature as well as answers to specific questions, such as which of the three tax forms — 1040EZ, 1040A or 1040 — you should use. The Internal Revenue Service office is open from 8:30 a.m. to 5 p.m. and provides assistance and answers to specific questions regarding the arcana of calculating your Federal income tax, but they will not do it for you.

Illinois income tax forms can be obtained at the State of Illinois Building, 100 West Randolph Street, in the lobby or at the Department of Revenue offices, 230 South Dearborn Street, 8:30 a.m. to 5 p.m., or you can call 800-732-8866 or 312-814-5232. The basic form is the IL-1040, the Illinois Individual Income Tax Return. For individuals, the state income tax rate is 3%.

In Chicago, the sales tax rate is 8.75% (5% for the state, 2% for the city, 1% for the RTA, and .75% for Cook County).

YOU'RE SETTLED IN YOUR NEW APARTMENT. YOU HAVE ELECTRICity, a phone and heat, but now your personal needs are just beginning. Below are a few service suggestions to ease your exciting transition into Chicago life.

## FURNITURE RENTAL

If you arrived in the Windy City unburdened with home furnishings and with no intention of acquiring these bothersome but necessary items, there are businesses that will cater to your lean and free-spirited nature. Most furniture-rental companies offer wide selection, flexible leases, purchase options (rental payments may apply toward purchase in some cases), and quick delivery.

- **Brook Furniture Rental** has four Chicago-area locations: Downtown, 208 South LaSalle Street, 312-939-0051; Deerfield, 20510 North Milwaukee Avenue, 847-945-6696; Elk Grove Village, 2301 East Oakton, 847-593-0170; Downers Grove, 1915 Ogden, 630-963-1819.
- **Cort Furniture Rental**, 22 West Ontario Street, 312-266-8719, leases home and office furniture. Cort also has a suburban showrooms in Arlington Heights, 955 East Algonquin Road, 847-981-1450.
- **Instant Interiors**, 446 East Ontario Street, 312-951-5024
- **Swingles Furniture Rental**, 2461 Oakton, Elk Grove Village, 800-560-2111

## TELEVISION AND VCR RENTAL

As with furniture, if you rent your television, VCR, stereo or any other appliances, various rental plans are available with rent-to-own options.

Some agencies will include free service, so be sure to ask.

- **Rent-a-Center**, has twelve locations in Chicago, including 6718 North Clark Street, 773-973-7500, and 3059 North Pulaski Road, 773-202-9090. Rent-a-Center will rent to you by the day, week, month or to own with no credit check, no deposit and no long-term obligation.
- **Remco** has brand-name televisions, stereos and other appliances either for rent or rent-to-own (free service while you rent to own). Remco has five locations throughout Chicago and suburbs, including 2595 North Elston Avenue, 773-395-4900; 3145 South Ashland Avenue, 773-376-4200; 3214 North Kimball Avenue, 773-478-0950.

## COMPUTER RENTAL

In a city as business-oriented as Chicago, computer rental agencies abound. Check to see whether service is included and whether the company has a 24-hour hotline for service calls. The following is a brief list to start your search.

- **Abacus**, 1165 Tower Road, Schaumburg, 847-882-2030, offers: Compaq and IBM.
- **Computerland**, 150 North Wacker Drive, 312-236-9400, offers: Compaq, HP, IBM, Macintosh.
- **Datasis Corporation**, 1687 Elmhurst Road., Elk Grove Village, 847-427-0909, offers: Compaq, IBM and Macintosh.
- **Microage Computer Center** has two downtown and Near-North locations: 111 North Canal Street, 312-715-3100; and 343 West Erie Street, 312-266-8100.
- **Personal Computer Rental**, Elk Grove Village, 847-272-0042, offers: Compaq, IBM and Macintosh.

## HAIRCUTS

A haircut is a personal thing, and if you had someone cutting your hair where you used to live who knew you, knew your personality and knew your head, they were probably tough to leave. Now that you're in a new city ask a friend or co-worker for the name of someone they like, and remember it may take some time for you to find the right person for your hair; until then, here are a few suggestions.

- **SuperCuts** is a good choice if you have relatively hassle-free hair. Their cutters can give you a decent "do" for less than $14. Each salon is an independently owned franchise; the price, walk-in policy and satisfaction guarantee have made them popular. If you're unhappy with your haircut, SuperCuts guarantees that you can have your hair recut or your money returned within seven days, no questions asked. SuperCuts are located throughout the city, including downtown at 100 West Randolph Street, 312-419-1799, and 336 South Michigan Avenue, 312-341-9797; on the North Side at 1628 North Wells Street, 312-944-7778; 1353 West Fullerton Avenue, 773-281-3030; 3160 North Broadway, 773-935-5252; 2912 North Ashland Avenue, 773-525-5445; and in Hyde Park at 1644 East 53rd Street, 773-955-0100. Hours vary from salon to salon, but many are open week nights until 9 p.m.

- **Eclipse Artistic Hair Group**, 2535 North Lincoln Avenue, 773-348-6522, offers all hair, nail and skin services with an attractive combination of late hours and reliable service. Eclipse is open Monday through Thursday, 12 p.m. to 9 p.m., Friday 12 p.m. to 8 p.m., Saturday 9 a.m. to 6 p.m. and Sunday from 12 p.m. to 5 p.m. Men's cuts are $32-36, women's $42-49.

- **Elizabeth Adam Salon**, 70 East Walton Street, 312-642-6640, is located in the heart of Chicago's high-fashion shopping district. Elizabeth Adam is a true beauty salon devoted to hair care, makeup and pampering. Before your first visit, the manager will take the time (over the phone or in person) to match your tastes with a member of the talented, diverse staff. The salon specializes in coloring, but also offers haircuts, perms and styling, a full makeup line and makeup artist, as well as manicures and private pedicures. The atmosphere is chic and the staff attentive, but you pay for the service. Haircuts range from $45 to $110, depending on the stylist; perms begin at $85; highlighting ranges from $75 to $140; facials start at $60; and manicures are $16. Prices are slightly lower for men. Hours are 8:00 a.m. to 7:00 p.m. Monday through Saturday.

- **Sine Qua Non Hair Design**, 2944 North Lincoln Avenue, 773-871-2280, is an Aveda Concept Salon (which means it only uses, and retails, Aveda products). The cuts here are chic and the staff and decor make you feel great; caters to a hip, slightly upscale crowd. Located in Lakeview, but conveniently close to Lincoln Park and DePaul, the evening hours are particularly convenient for daytime toilers. Hours: Monday, 12 p.m. to 8 p.m.; Tuesday, Wednesday, Thursday, 1 p.m. to 9 p.m.; Friday 11 a.m. to 7 p.m.; and Saturday, 9 a.m. to 5 p.m. Women's cuts are $30-$45, men's $20-$32.

## HOUSECLEANING

If you can afford it, maid service will keep your weekends free for recreation and not the Saturday chores. There is all manner of maid service, and they'll come weekly, semi-weekly, monthly — whatever you need. And they do windows. Make sure your service is bonded and insured. Here are few suggestions for places to start looking for a cleaning service:

- **Brooms Unlimited,** 10 West Kinzie Street, 773-549-4258
- **Cleaning Club,** 2121 North Clybourn Avenue, 773-477-1133
- **Heaven-Sent Housekeepers,** 2620 North Wayne Avenue, 773-348-1107
- **Lake Shore Condo Cleaners,** 3550 North Lake Shore Drive, 773-549-5765
- **Mighty Maids,** 2950 North Sheffield Avenue, 773-472-7711
- **North Shore Maids,** 3525 West Peterson Avenue, 773-509-1200

You also may consider asking your landlord if he knows an independent housecleaner who works regularly in your building or neighborhood.

## MAIL AND TELEPHONE

If you haven't yet found an apartment or are frequently out of town and want to keep in touch, old fashioned telephone answering services, with live human beings, will answer the phone for you while you are gone. You can also rent a mailbox at a neighborhood post office or an independent mailbox service (usually more expensive than the USPS).

- **United States Postal Service,** call the main post office downtown ("the central facility") for postal information, 312-983-8400.

- **Mail Boxes Etc.** has several centers at convenient locations:
  60 East Chestnut, 312-787-7277.
  858 West Armitage Avenue, 773-528-0011
  2506 North Clark Street, 773-935-7755
  3023 North Clark Street, 773-281-8988
  3712 North Broadway, 773-975-7100
  1507 East 53rd Street, 773-288-3173

Telephone answering services are ubiquitous and offer many services — message service, paging, voice mail, even wake-up calls —

depending upon your needs. There is an extensive listing in the Yellow Pages under "Telephone Answering Service." You might consider:

- **A-Around the Clock Answering Service**, 773-545-6066
- **Ameritech**, 1-800-660-3000 (voice-mail)
- **Chicago Communications Service Inc.**, 312-829-2700
- **Chicagoland Answering Service**, 800-809-5700

## MOVING AND STORAGE

There are storage warehouses aplenty in Chicago. Just check the Yellow Pages under "Storage - Household & Commercial" for complete listings. Prices and options vary; call around and ask questions. For example, what kind of security arrangements does the space have? When do you have access? Is the facility heated and/or air-conditioned? Does the location have sprinklers in case of fire? Are there carts and hand trucks for moving in and out? Do you have to write a check each month, or will they automatically charge the bill to your credit card? Here are a few suggestions (although where you live and where they are located will surely be important to you):

- **The Cache**, 3800 North Sheffield Avenue, 773-248-5005
- **Chicago Lock Stock & Storage**, 2001 North Elston Avenue, 773-227-2448
- **East Bank Self-Storage and Truck Rental**, 429 West Ohio Street, 312-644-2000
- **Public Storage** has more than 50 storage facilities in the Chicago metropolitan area. Check the Yellow Pages or call 1-800-447-8673 for the location nearest you.
- **Strongbox** has two Chicago locations - 1516 North Orleans Street, 312-787-2800, and 1650 West Irving Park Road, 773-248-6800.
- **U-Haul Self-Storage** has storage facilities throughout the Chicago metropolitan area. In Chicago, check out those at 1200 West Fullerton Avenue, 773-935-0620, and 4055 North Broadway, 773-871-7155. Check the Yellow Pages for other locations.

N AN EFFORT TO KEEP SHOPPING FOR YOUR NEW PLACE TO A minimum number of stops, we offer a list of full-service department stores where you can do most of your shopping, followed by more specialized stores that offer a wider selection of hard-to-find items.

## FULL-SERVICE DEPARTMENT STORES

- **Carson Pirie Scott & Company** offers everything from clothing and furniture to bridal wear to stamps and coins to …. Carson's has stores throughout Chicago and the suburbs, including the flagship store at 1 South State Street, 312-641-7000, and a second city location at Gateway Shops, 120 South Riverside Plaza, 312-744-5380. Suburban locations include Evergreen Park, 9700 South Western Avenue, 708-636-1000; Yorktown, Wolf Road and the Eisenhower Expressway, 630-620-2600; Lincolnwood Town Center, 3333 West Touhy Avenue, 847-982-0600; North Riverside, 7505 West Cermak Road, 708-442-6200; and Edens Plaza in Wilmette, 3200 Lake Avenue, 847-251-8400.
- **Marshall Field's** is a Chicago institution that offers everything — from designer clothing to gourmet food to home furnishings — but friendly service. Visitors come from around the country to see the store's Christmas window displays at the beautifully renovated State Street store. The flagship store is at 111 North State Street (in the Loop), 312-781-1000, and there is one in the glamorous Water Tower Place vertical mall, 835 North Michigan Avenue, 312-335-7700. Suburban locations include Lake Forest, 682 North Bank Lane, 847-735-2100; Oak Brook, 1 Oak Brook Center Mall, 630-684-2400; and Schaumburg, 1 Woodfield Mall, 847-706-6000.
- **Montgomery Ward**, another, albeit struggling, Chicago institution, has locations at 2939 West Addison Street, 773-267-4092; 6525 West Diversey Parkway, 773-745-1300; 7601 South Cicero Avenue, 773-284-4800; 4620 South Damen Avenue, 773-650-1090

- **Sears,** 1601 North Harlem Avenue, 773-804-5000; 4730 West Irving Park Road, 773-202-2000; 1900 West Lawrence Avenue, 773-769-8030; 1334 East 79th Street, 773-933-1600; 6153 South Western Avenue, 773-918-1400; and 7601 South Cicero Avenue, 773-284-4200.

North Michigan Avenue, Chicago's glitzy and expensive Magnificent Mile, has dozens of large stores and several highrise shopping malls that you may want to consider.

- **Henri Bendel,** 900 North Michigan Avenue, 312-642-0140
- **Bloomingdale's,** 900 North Michigan Avenue, 312-440-4460
- **Lord & Taylor,** 835 North Michigan Avenue, 312-787-7400
- **Neiman Marcus,** 737 North Michigan Avenue, 312- 642-5900
- **Saks Fifth Avenue,** 700 North Michigan Avenue, 312-944-6500

When shopping the Magnificent Mile, be sure to swing down to the newly renovated State Street shopping area. In an effort to get people back to this once popular shopping destination, the city routed car traffic back down State Street, which was previously reserved for buses only. The hope was that if people traveling through this area, whether by bus, taxi or car, could see the storefronts, there would be a renewed interest in shopping here. It's been very effective and the street is especially popular during the summer and Christmas seasons. State Street is now a lovely, bustling reminder of a turn of the century gas light shopping district, complete with the grandeur of the original Marshall Field's and Carson Pirie Scott Department stores.

Chicago also has many fine shopping malls in the city and suburbs.

## SHOPPING MALLS

### CHICAGO

- **The Atrium,** 100 West Randolph Street, 312-346-0777
- **The Brickyard,** 6465 West Diversey Parkway, 773-745-8838
- **The Century,** 2828 North Clark Street, 773-929-8100
- **Ford City,** 7601 South Cicero Avenue, 773-767-6400
- **Harper Court,** 5211-25 South Harper Avenue, 773-363-8282
- **Chicago Place,** 700 North Michigan Avenue, 312-642-4811
- **Water Tower Place,** 835 North Michigan Avenue, 312-440-3165

## SUBURBS

- **Edens Plaza,** Lake Avenue & Skokie Boulevard, Wilmette, 847-256-9157
- **Evergreen Plaza**, 9500 South Western Avenue, Evergreen Park, 773-445-8900
- **Golf Mill Shopping Center**, Golf & Milwaukee Roads, Niles, 847-699-1070
- **Northbrook Court**, 2171 Northbrook Court, Northbrook, 847-498-5144
- **Oak Brook Center**, Route 83 and Cermak Road, Oak Brook, 630-573-0250
- **Old Orchard**, Skokie Boulevard & Old Orchard Road, Skokie, 847-673-6800
- **Plaza del Lago**, 1515 Sheridan Road, Wilmette, 847-256-4467
- **Randhurst Shopping Center**, 999 Elmhurst Road, Mt. Prospect, 708-259-0500
- **Stratford Square,** Army Trail Road & Gary, 630-351-9405
- **Yorktown Shopping Center**, Butterfield Road & Highland, Lombard, 630-629-7330

### BEDS AND BEDDING

- **Arise Futon**, 3152 North Lincoln Avenue, 312-280-2311
- **Arrelle Fine Linens & Down**, 445 North Wells Street, 312-321-3696
- **Futonair**, 3162 North Clark Street, 773-281-0215
- **Jennifer Convertibles** has four locations: 180 North Wabash Avenue, 312-553-0260; 814 West North Avenue, 312-951-9377; 730 West Diversey Parkway, 773-281-9991; and 2907 West Addison Street, 773-583-2171.
- **Private Lives,** Chicago's largest selection of bed and bed linen, has locations at 56 East Oak Street, 312-337-5474, and 622 West Diversey Parkway, 773-525-6464.

### CAMERAS, ELECTRONICS AND APPLIANCES

- **Best Buy** is a warehouse-style store with a huge selection and good prices. You definitely won't be pestered by salespeople here; in fact, it may be hard to find them. The Chicago store is located at 1000 West North Avenue, 312-988-4067. Suburban sites include: Evanston, 2301 Howard Street, 847-570-0450; and Skokie, 5425

Touhy Avenue, 847-933-9170.
- **The Camera Network**, 1000 North Halsted Street, 312-867-8777
- **Central Camera**, 230 South Wabash Avenue, 312-427-5580
- **Circuit City**, 2500 North Elston, 773-772-0037
- **Hammacher Schlemmer & Co.** (an eclectic collection of things you never knew you didn't have), 445 North Michigan Avenue, 312-527-9100.
- **Helix Camera & Video** has Loop and Near West Side locations: Main Store (the largest camera store in the United States), 310 South Racine Avenue, 312-421-6000; 2 Illinois Center, 312-565-5901; 3 First National Plaza, 312-444-9373.
- **Mid-State Camera Service** (for camera repair), 407 S. Dearborn, #300, 312-939-2272.
- **Montgomery Ward & Co. Electric Avenue** stores include 825 West North Avenue, 915-0030; 2939 West Addison Street, 509-2800; North Riverside, 7503 West Cermak Road, 708-442-6100.
- **Shutan Camera & Video**, 312 West Randolph Street, 312-332-2000
- **United Audio Center** has three Chicago-area locations: 900 North Michigan Avenue, 312-664-3100; The Century Shopping Center (level 4), 2828 North Clark Street, 773-525-7005; and Edens Plaza in Wilmette, 847-251-1860.
- **Wolf Camera & Video** has locations throughout the Chicago metropolitan area. In Chicago: 66 East Madison Street, 312-346-2288; 750 North Rush Street, 312-943-5531; and 1919 North Clybourn Avenue, 773-528-5585. Evanston, 616 Davis Street, 847-328-0111. Oak Park, 135 North Oak Park Avenue, 708-848-2451. Skokie, 7933 North Lincoln Avenue, 847-673-2530.

## CARPETS AND RUGS

- **Caspian Oriental Rugs**, 700 North LaSalle Street, 312-664-7576
- **Home Carpet & Linoleum Center**, 3071 North Lincoln Avenue, 773-935-9314
- **Peerless Imported Rugs**, 3033 North Lincoln Avenue, 773-525-9034
- **Rexx Rug & Linoleum Co.**, 3312 North Lincoln Avenue, 773-281-8800, Rexx Rug has a large discounted inventory of carpeting for immediate installation.

## COMPUTER EQUIPMENT

The listings for computer sales and support go on for pages in the Yellow Pages under "Computers."

- **C. D. Warehouse**, 315 Grand Avenue, 312-527-2700
- **Comp USA**, 101 East Chicago Avenue, 312-787-6776
- **Comp USA**, 7011 Central Avenue, Skokie, 847-677-3644
- **Hyde Park Computers, Inc.** , 2850 North Clark Street, 773-248-6200; 1466 East 53rd Street, 773-288-5971
- **MicroAge Computer Center**, 111 North Canal Street, 312-715-3100
- **Micro Center**, 2645 North Elston Avenue, 773-292-1700

## DISCOUNT STORES

- **K-Mart**, 6211 North Lincoln Avenue, 773-267-2441; 3443 West Addison Street, 773-478-1334; 1360 North Ashland Avenue, 773-292-9400; 6435 West Diversey Parkway, 773-745-8350; 5050 South Kedzie Avenue, 773-476-7887; 7050 South Pulaski Road, 773-767-2800
- **Service Merchandise** has two Chicago stores at 3240 North Ashland Avenue, 773-472-3940, and 3620 East 118th Street, 773-646-5296. They offer a wide variety of small appliances, electronics, and household goods. They also have an extensive jewelry selection.
- **Target** now has two stores in the Chicago area and is an excellent choice for reasonably-priced lighting, smaller furniture, kitchen wares, clothing, simple electronics, and, of course, the irresistibly priced package of 200 rolls of toilet paper. Now if you can only figure out how to get it to the car . . . The Chicago store is at 2656 North Elston Avenue, 773-252-1994; the Evanston store is at 2209 West Howard Street, 847-733-1144.

## FURNITURE

Chicago has furniture stores to accommodate every taste and pocketbook.

- **Affordable Portables** located at 2608-10 North Clark Street, 773-935-6160, and Evanston, 924 Davis Street, 847-866-8124.
- **Crate & Barrel**, a notable company that has continued to improve its merchandise and selection, has stores in the city and suburbs that offer contemporary furniture and household accessories,

including an outlet store where you can pick up some wonderful items at bargain prices. Crate & Barrel stores are located at 646 North Michigan Avenue, 312-787-5900; 101 North Wabash Avenue, 312-372-0100; 1515 Sheridan Road, Wilmette, 847-256-2726; 54 Oak Brook Center Mall, Oak Brook, 630-572-9199; and the outlet store, 800 West North Avenue, 312-787-4775.

- **The Container Store**, 908 North Avenue, 312-654-8450, though not a true furniture store, promises Chicagoans with money that most precious of urban commodities: more efficient (and stylish) use of scarce living space.
- **European Furniture Warehouse**, 2145 West Grand Avenue, 312-243-1955
- **The Great Ace** has furniture, bedding and an excellent hardware department. Located in Webster Place, a mall at the southwest corner of Webster & Clybourn Avenues, 773-348-0705.
- **Homemakers Furniture, Inc.**, 825 West North Avenue, 312-649-5500, also has locations in the following suburbs: Schaumburg, 1733 Woodfield Road (opposite Woodfield Shopping Center), 847-619-6800; Downers Grove, 1013 Butterfield Road, 630-852-6880; and Orland Park, 66 Orland Square Drive, 708-349-5800.
- **Naked Furniture**, 5725 North Broadway, 773-784-1616
- **Pier 1 Imports, Inc.**, has many locations, including: 1350 North Wells Street, 312-787-4320; 2112 North Clybourn Avenue, 773-871-6610; 651 West Diversey Parkway, 773-871-1558; and 2868 North Ashland Avenue, 773-975-1033.
- **Scandinavian Design**, 4028 Dempster, Skokie, 847-568-0500

## GROCERY STORES

The dominant grocery store chains in Chicago are Dominick's and Jewel. If you're looking for that tough-to-find *fromage* or pasta, try Treasure Island. If you've jumped on the organic bandwagon, there's Whole Foods. If you want to buy in bulk, Cub Foods or Sam's Club is a good bet.

- **Cub Foods**, 2627 North Elston Avenue, 773-252-6400
- **Dominick's** has many Chicago locations, including 3012 North Broadway, 773-549-6100; 3350 North Western Avenue, 773-929-8910; 5235 North Sheridan Road, 773-728-4300; and 6009 North Broadway, 773-769-2300.
- **Jewel** has scores of stores in and around Chicago, including 1210

North Clark Street, 312-944-6950; 3033 South Halsted, 312-225-1010; 1240 West Harrison Street, 312-243-2370; 3531 North Broadway, 773-871-1054; 1341 North Paulina Street, 773-342-3410; 3630 North Southport Avenue, 773-281-1521; 7536 North Western Avenue, 773-743-8315; 438 West Madison, Oak Park, 708-383-7111.

- **Sam's Club,** 2450 Main Street, Evanston, 847-491-9000
- **Treasure Island** has four locations: 75 West Elm Street, 312-440-1144; 1639 North Wells Street, 312-642-1105; 3460 North Broadway, 773-327-3880; and 2121 North Clybourn Avenue, 773-880-8880.
- **Whole Foods,** health and organic food, deli, baked goods. The North Avenue location has an excellent cafe on the upper level. 1000 West North Avenue, 312-587-0648; 3300 North Ashland Avenue, 773-244-4200.

If you're looking for especially fresh produce, the City of Chicago sponsors **farmers' markets** during the summer in locations throughout the city, including Daley Plaza in the Loop. Try Lincoln Park High School's parking lot on Armitage Avenue east of Halsted Street on Saturday morning. Further north, visit the one in Lincoln Square (just south of Lawrence Avenue on Lincoln Avenue) which is held every Tuesday morning. For a list of other market locations and dates, call 312-744-9187.

For those internet junkies who cannot leave their computer to venture out for sustenance, or if you just don't like crowded Saturday morning shopping, for a price, there is an online shopping service in town called **Peapod**. Their software is user-friendly and they deliver. Call 800-5PEAPOD or visit their site at *www.peapod.com* for details.

## HARDWARE, PAINTS, AND WALLPAPER

Hardware stores can be found in every neighborhood. Chicago's biggest chains are ACE and True Value.

- **ACE Hardware** locations include 4654 North Broadway, 773-334-7146; 1304 East 53rd Street, 773-493-1700; Ashland Paint & Hardware, 1013 North Ashland Avenue, 773-486-1271; Imperial ACE Hardware, 1208 West Grand Avenue, 312-421-0475; Lakeview ACE Hardware, 3921 North Sheridan Road, 773- 525-1700; Meyer's ACE Hardware, 315 East 35th Street, 312-225-5687; Ravenswood

ACE Hardware, 1953 West Lawrence Avenue, 773-561-5228; Stauber ACE Hardware, 3911 North Lincoln Avenue, 773-281-1777; and Streeterville ACE Hardware, 680 North Lake Shore Drive, 312-266-0900.

- **True Value Hardware** locations include Charles Variety & True Value Stores, Inc., 1516 West Morse Avenue, 773-761-2298; Clark-Devon Hardware, 6401 North Clark Street, 773-764-3575; Edward's True Value Hardware, 2804 North Halsted Street, 773-525-6104; Klein True Value Hardware, 3737 North Southport Avenue, 773-525-2291; Lehman's True Value Hardware, 3473 North Broadway, 773-472-4435; Roscoe Hardware Co., 2032 West Roscoe Street, 773-348-0394; Tenenbaum H.A. Hardware Company, 1138 West Belmont Avenue, 773-935-7374; and Wahler Brothers True Value Hardware, 2551 North Halsted Street, 773-248-1349.
- **Home Depot,** 1232 West North Avenue, 773-486-9200; 7200 South Cicero Avenue, 773-586-0032; 2201 Oakton, Evanston, 847-733-9200, is perfect for do-it-yourself home repair as well as the professional contractor. It has an extensive garden center for spring and fall landscaping.

## SECOND-HAND SHOPPING

There are three kinds of second-hand stores: thrift stores, where the merchandise is cheap but not necessarily trendy; vintage stores, where the clothes are more fashionable and more expensive; and antiques stores where the merchandise may be exquisite, with prices to match. You can find forgotten gems at thrift stores (the exciting challenge) but you'll have to dig through a lot of dreck along the way. At vintage and antique stores that work is done for you but you pay the price.

## ANTIQUE STORES

There are plenty of opportunities to do antique shopping around Chicago, from auctions and galleries to antique warehouses. Be sure to call and inquire about store hours before dropping in; many shops keep odd hours and some serve by appointment only. Listed below are a few of the main antique stores and malls. Check the Yellow Pages under "Antiques" for more listings.

- **Antique House,** 1832 West Belmont Avenue, 773-327-0707

- **Antique Mall of Wrigleyville,** 3336 North Clark Street, 773-868-0285
- **Antiques at the Lincoln Mall,** 3141 North Lincoln Avenue, 773-244-1440
- **Armitage Antique Gallery,** 1539 West Armitage Avenue, 773-227-7727
- **Christa's Ltd.,** 217 West Illinois Street, 312 222-2520
- **Jay Robert's Antique Warehouse,** 149 West Kinzie Street, 312-222-0167
- **Ziggurat,** 1702 North Milwaukee Avenue, 773-227-6290

## VINTAGE STORES

- **Betty's Resale Shop,** 3439 North Lincoln Avenue, 773-929-6143
- **Dandelion,** 2117 North Damen Avenue, 773-862-9333
- **Disgraceland,** 3330 North Clark Street, 773-281-5875
- **Flashy Trash,** 3524 North Halsted Street, 773-327-6900
- **Hollywood Mirror,** 812 West Belmont, 773-404-4510
- **George's Antiques and Vintage,** 5308 North Clark Street, 773-784-7080
- **Hubba-Hubba,** 3338 North Clark Street, 773-477-1414
- **Silver Moon,** 3337 North Halsted Street, 773-883-0222
- **Strange Cargo,** 3448 North Clark Street, 773-327-8090
- **Wacky Cats,** 3109 North Lincoln Avenue, 773-929-6701
- **Wild Thing,** 2933 North Clark Street, 773-549-7787

## THRIFT STORES

- **Brown Elephant Resale Shop** for the Howard Brown Memorial Clinic, 3651 North Halsted Street, 773-549-5943.
- **The Salvation Army** operates more than a dozen thrift shops in Chicago. Check out 2270 North Clybourn Avenue, 773-477-1300; 3868 North Lincoln Avenue, 773-528-8893; or 2151 West Devon Avenue, 773-262-3645. For other locations look in the Yellow Pages under Thrift Shops.
- **Unique Thrift,** 3224 South Halsted Street, 773-842-8123; 4112 North Lincoln Avenue, 773-281-1590; 4445 North Sheridan Road, 773-275-8623
- **Village Discount Outlet** has stores throughout Chicago including, 2032 North Milwaukee Avenue, 2855 North Halsted Street, 4898 North Clark Street, and 2043 West Roscoe Street. Same number for

all stores: 708-388-4772.
- **White Elephant Shop of Children's Memorial Hospital**, 2380 North Lincoln Avenue, 773-281-3747

## DUMPSTER DIVING
*(also known as Alley Shopping)*

Many a funky Chicago apartment has been accented, or even primarily outfitted, with recycled material from alleys and dumpsters. Every neighborhood has a specific day for garbage pickup and the ideal time to go scrounging is the day or morning, before the blue Streets & Sanitation trucks cart it all away. The best times of the year to go hunting are the last weekends of April and September, when many leases expire and the alleys are piled high with whatever didn't make the cut. But the pickings are good at the end of any month. Another rewarding time to covet thy neighbor's trash is in springtime when people clean out their garages, basements, attics, etc. All in all, the alleys of Chicago offer the widest possible selection of used furniture, appliances, and household and decorative items at the lowest possible prices. Look out your back window for the one nearest you.

## SPORTING GOODS

- **Active Endeavors**, 935 West Armitage Avenue, 773-281-8100; 1527 Chicago Avenue, Evanston, 847-869-7070
- **Sportmart**, 440 North Orleans Street, 312-527-3516; 620 North LaSalle Street, 312-337-6151; 3134 North Clark Street, 773-871-8500; and 6420 West Fullerton Avenue, 773-804-0044
- **Vertel's Chicago Running Athletics and Fitness**, 2001 North Clybourn Avenue, 773-248-7400

## CONSUMER COMPLAINTS

A final note, if you feel you have been cheated in some way by a merchant or retailer in the city of Chicago you can call the **Chicago Department of Consumer Services**, 312-744-9400, to file a complaint. Included within their jurisdiction are apartment problems, food related issues and auto dealers.

## CHILD CARE

Q UALITY CHILD CARE EXISTS IN CHICAGO. THE PROBLEM IS finding it. To begin with, there are so many options — daycare centers, child care homes, group child care homes, nannies, au pairs, babysitters — it's enough to give any concerned parent a headache. Add to that the difficulty of deciding which of these is the right one for you and your child. Compound this with the hard work of finding that one ideal provider. Finally, blend it all in with the frustration of being put on a two to three year waiting list, and you'll begin to understand the frustration of Chicago parents.

To help make things easier, talk to those who have been in your shoes; friends or co-workers with children often have the best suggestions for finding good child care. Beyond that it's helpful to familiarize yourself with the local child care scene and the different options available to you.

## DAYCARE

Looking for the right person or center to care for your child is one of the most difficult and anxiety ridden tasks a parent will undertake. Listed below are several daycare options including daycare centers, in-home child care, nannies and au pairs. One big issue to consider before embarking on this difficult task is the cost of daycare, which can range from $4,000 to $15,000 a year for full-time infant care, and from $3,500 to $8,000 a year for full-time preschool care. Be aware that Chicago does not permit infants younger than three months into daycare centers.

As you begin your search you will realize that there are many options available. However, if you are new in town without the benefit of family or close friends who can recommend a daycare provider or offer their own services, your best choice may be to narrow your search to licensed providers. The state divides daycare facilities into the following four categories (always ask the daycare provider if they are licensed by the state):

**Child Care Homes** are smaller facilities (eight or fewer children) which are run out of the house of the provider. The care here is more individualized and the setting more familiar than the larger centers, and the prices tend to be lower. Though some may advertise in neighborhood papers, many get their business through word of mouth; ask around your neighborhood or at work.

**Group Child Care Homes** are also run out of the house of the provider, but the number of children allowed is greater (up to twelve).

**Child Care Centers** are what most people think of when they think "daycare." These are larger, more school-like facilities which offer constant supervision and tend to be around longer, though the staff may change. Because of the number of employees and the higher overhead required to operate a separate building, the prices are higher than daycare homes. Frequently there are waiting lists to get in.

**License Exempt Child Care** facilities are either too small (three children or fewer) to be regulated or are operated by non-profit organizations such as churches.

Licensing for daycare centers in Illinois require that the care givers have a minimum of six hours of college credit in child development as well as a minimum of 15 clock hours of on site training. Directors are required to have two years of college credit with 18 semester hours in courses specifically related to young children. After passing an on site inspection for licensing, all daycare facilities are then inspected once a year.

*Remember that parents or guardians have the right to visit homes or centers without prior notice anytime their children are in care.*

For more information about licensing laws and requirements contact the **Department of Children and Family Services**, 406 East Monroe Street, Springfield, IL 62701, 217-785-2688.

For a list of licensed (and license exempt) providers call **Cook County Childcare Resource and Referral** at 773-769-8000. They will send you a free booklet detailing the child care options available in Cook County. They can also help you narrow the search down to those facilities in your own zip code, or adjoining ones. There are many listings in the Yellow Pages under "Child Care" but the simple fact that a provider is in the Yellow Pages is no guarantee that the service is licensed or reputable.

Finally, you might check with your local **church** or **synagogue**. Many religious institutions offer excellent daycare and you do not necessarily have to be a member of the flock to take advantage of a house of worship's childcare service. Universities, too, may offer quality pre-school with fees on a sliding scale for the children of parents who are attending classes.

## NANNIES

Hiring a nanny is usually the most expensive daycare option. Recently, the going rate in Chicago was $200 to $400 per week. Nannies with substantial experience charge the most, sometimes above $400 per week. But having a nanny offers your child (or children) a level of personal attention which daycare can't match. The trick is finding a qualified person. Unfortunately, at the present time, there is no national licensing or certification program for nannies. This means it's up to you to determine if the person is qualified. There are some bottom line questions that you'll want to know the answers to: Do they speak English? Can they legally work in the U.S.? How extensive is their child care experience? You'll also want to talk to all their references. Services you can use to investigate prospective nannies include:

**Infotrack Information Services, Inc.**, 925 North Milwaukee Avenue, #224, Wheeling, IL 60090, 708-808-9990, 800-275-5594, is a private investigative company that conducts background investigations for pre-employment screenings. They check for a driving record, criminal record and do a credit report at a cost of $40.

**Verified Credentials, Inc.** 1020 East 146th Street, #200, Burnsville, MN 55337, 612-431-1811, is a background-check agency specializing in pre-employment screening. The company works with nanny placement agencies and nanny employers. They check for a driving record, criminal record and do a credit report at a cost of $40.

**Employment Screening Network,** 129 East Main Street, Westminster, MD 21157, is a private investigative company that provides employers with pre-employment investigations and has been conducting checks on nannies since 1987. Their basic package includes criminal record check, a check on where the candidate has lived in the past seven years, an interview with the candidate's last employer and job application checks. The cost is $50 - $200.

Nannies advertise, but not in obvious places. Instead of the *Tribune* or *Sun-Times*, look in the classified section of your local neighborhood newspaper or *Chicago Parent* magazine. Or look on the bulletin board of your local church or grocery store. Better yet, ask neighbors, friends, and colleagues for recommendations.

If all this is starting to sound like a lot of work, there is another way. A nanny service will do the search for you *but* you should ask some questions of them before you hire them; you will be paying a lot for the service (prices range from $1,000 to $2,000) so better safe than sorry. Do they screen their nannies and what are the screening criteria? Will you get to interview any and all candidates face to face? What happens to the finder's fee if the nanny doesn't work out?

Look under "Nanny Services" in the Yellow Pages for a list of providers. Who knows? You might wind up with the next Mary Poppins.

## AU PAIRS

The U.S. Information Agency oversees and approves the organizations which offer this service. Younger women (between 18-25) provide a year of in-home child care and light housekeeping in exchange for airfare, room and board, and a small stipend ($110 to $120 per week). The program is certainly valuable for the cultural exchange that goes on between the host family and the (usually European) au pair. The downside is that the program only lasts one year and the au pairs don't have the life or work experience of a career nanny. Any of the following national agencies will connect you with a local coordinator who will match up your family with the right au pair.

- **EF Au Pair**, 800-333-6056
- **Au Pair Homestay**, 800-479-0907
- **Au Pair International**, 800-654-2051
- **Au Pair in America**, 800-928-7247
- **Au Pair USA**, 800-287-2477

## BABYSITTING

Once again, the best way to find a competent reliable babysitter is to ask your neighbors and colleagues for recommendations. In Chicago, the high school or college babysitter earns between $5 and $10 per hour (depending on the number of children). Nanny services can also find a babysitter, but you'll pay more than you would for a neighborhood teenager. If you're looking for an older sitter you might consider calling the job referral service (or campus employment office) at a local college or university.

They can hook you up with college students who are looking for occasional babysitting jobs. Finally, you can call the **American Registry for Nurses and Sitters**, 773-248-8100. They will provide qualified sitters who have all undergone an extensive screening process. Residential rates are $10/hr. (with a four hour minimum). They will also provide babysitters for Chicago area hotels, though the rates there are higher.

## GENERAL RESOURCES

The **Northside Parents Network** (312-409-2233) is a group of around 200 parents that offers babysitting co-ops, playgroups, a new moms group, and parenting advice. They put out a newsletter as well as an excellent information booklet which profiles local schools (both public and private).

*Chicago Parent* magazine is another good place to look. It provides information on Chicago daycare centers as well as other programs that might be of interest to you or your child. It is published monthly and distributed free of charge at libraries, park districts, and book and toy stores throughout the city. You can also subscribe by calling 708-386-5555.

## SCHOOLS

For many years, public schools in Chicago were reputed to be among the worst in the country: test scores were low, classes were crowded, hallways were dangerous, and public confidence in the system was marginal at best. Recently, however, wrenching reforms initiated by the city and state have shaken things up, and, though it's still too early to say for sure, some believe public schools have begun to improve. Only time will tell. It's not surprising then that many concerned parents turn to private and religious schools rather than risk their child's future on a substandard education. What may be surprising, though, is that some public schools are excellent, with long waiting lists to get in.

## PUBLIC SCHOOLS

In an effort to decentralize and invigorate the entire school system while, at the same time, making individual schools more accountable to parents and the surrounding community, every public school is now governed by a Local School Council (LSC). Composed of teachers, parents, and local residents these LSCs meet throughout the school year and are excellent places to get a feel for the school and observe its inner workings. For the local school in your area call the **Chicago Board of Education** at 773-535-4357.

To find out how a school's IGAP (annual state-sponsored standardized tests) scores compare to those of other schools keep an eye out in November: both the *Tribune* and *Sun-Times* publish a complete list of scores during that month. Most larger libraries have microfilm or CD-ROM archives of both these newspapers so you can check last year's score.

If your local school is not up to snuff, the next option may be magnet schools. These can be entire schools, programs within local schools, or academies. The categories get confusing, but the primary distinction between these and local schools is that they offer more services and in-depth learning. The waiting lists to get into many of these programs are daunting. A random lottery determines admission but some preference is given to those who already have siblings attending the school. An important note: the deadline for applying for the next school year is Jan. 15th. The Board of Education puts out an annual guide to different magnet schools and programs called "**Options for Knowledge.**" Call 312-535-7790 to get a free copy.

## PRIVATE, PAROCHIAL & RELIGIOUS SCHOOLS

Chicago has a large Catholic population and, as a result, a large number of Catholic schools: 146 grade schools and 29 high schools to be precise. But religion alone does not account for their popularity. To begin with, Catholic schools are cheaper than many other private schools and usually don't have a waiting list (except in southwest Chicago and Lake County). They also have a reputation for being safer and more disciplined than public schools. Non-Catholics are welcome and a surprising number do enroll their children in Catholic schools, especially grade schools. Generally, however, tuition for parishioners is lower than for non-parishioners. For information about Catholic schools in your area call the **Office of Catholic Education** at 312-751-5200. Test score information for schools is available on request by calling the individual school. These scores will be useful for comparing parochial schools to each other but not to other schools. The public school IGAP test is not administered in private schools.

If you're looking for religious schooling of a different stripe, rest assured that it's available. While the networks of other religious schools are less extensive, they offer the same advantages as Catholic schools. Talk to practitioners at your church or synagogue for recommendations and information.

Finally, private schools tend to offer the most costly programs but also some of the best. Options range from traditional college prep secondary schools to innovative programs for grade-schoolers. It's difficult to make generalizations about private schools because their curricula and teaching philosophies are so diverse. The best thing to do is check out different programs and see which feels right.

## RESOURCES

When it comes to getting information about schools, newcomers can find themselves in a real catch-22 — the best information you'll get will come from other parents, but the best way to meet other parents is through your child's school. Don't despair. For an excellent overview of the different choices available in Chicago, contact the **Northside Parents Network** at 312-409-2233. They put out an annual "School Information Booklet" ($5 for members/$12 for non-members) which lists different schools, defines technical terms, and offers guidelines for how to go about choosing the right school for your child. The booklet covers public, religious, and private schools. A more expensive solution, but perhaps one more tailored to your own particular situation, is to call **School Match** at 800-992-5323. For $97.50 they will send you a list of the top fifteen schools (public or private depending on your request) in your area which best suit your own requirements. These requirements are determined by filling out a questionnaire which you return to them.

## COLLEGES AND UNIVERSITIES

For the older or avid learner, Chicago offers a wide range of education options. Whether it's a doctorate in medieval history or a weekend pottery class, you can find it here. And everything in between of course. The following list of larger and better known institutions is far from comprehensive.

• **City Colleges of Chicago** (312-553-3300). Seven different campuses are scattered throughout the city. The majority of students are older or returning to school after being in the work force. A variety of two-year associate degrees are offered.

- **Columbia College** (312-663-1600) is located downtown across the street from the Art Institute and is best known as an art school. Enrollment has skyrocketed in recent years as a result of the college's open enrollment policy and its highly regarded programs in dance, film, and photography.
- **DePaul University** (312-362-8000) has two main campuses: one in Lincoln Park, the other in the Loop. Its business school and theater department are well known, and it is one of the largest Catholic universities in the world.
- **Loyola University** (773-274-3000) is Chicago's other major Catholic university. Founded in 1870, it is located on the lake in East Rogers Park. If you live on the far North Side, this is a convenient place to take classes.
- **Northeastern Illinois University** (773-583-4050). Primarily a comuter school, it is located in the northwestern part of the city. Northeastern is part of the state university system and is best known for its teacher training program.
- **Northwestern University** (847-491-7271) is a well regarded private university whose main campus is in leafy Evanston. The downtown Chicago campus is home to its Law, Medical and Dental Schools.
- **The School of the Art Institute of Chicago** (312-899-5219) is one of the nation's most highly regarded art schools. Though connected to the famous Art Institute museum, the course offerings aren't limited to painting and sculpture; performance art, video, and poetry are just some of the options.
- **The University of Chicago** (773-702-1234) is considered the area's premiere institution of higher learning. Located in Hyde Park, seven miles south of the Loop, its stern, gothic campus is home to more Nobel Prize winners than any educational institution in the country.
- **The University of Illinois at Chicago** (312-996-7000), better known as UIC, is located just west of downtown and offers a wide variety of degree programs. It has a large, modern, and growing campus and is convenient to public transit and all major expressways.

CHICAGO HAS AS DIVERSE AND VIBRANT A CULTURAL, INTELLECTUAL and artistic community as you will find anywhere in the world. From its world-class Chicago Symphony Orchestra to the esteemed Art Institute, Chicago is neither the Second nor the Third City when it comes to the arts.

If you want to find out what's going on when and where, here's a list of good places to start looking.

- *The Chicago Reader,* which comes out on Thursday nights, publishes a comprehensive entertainment guide of the coming week's concerts, performance art, drama, et al.
- *New City,* another alternative weekly, publishes an up-and-coming entertainment guide.

The *Chicago Sun-Times* and the *Chicago Tribune* publish entertainment guides on Friday and Sunday.

If you have thrown out the week's entertainment guide, there are several hotline numbers that you can call for the latest information on upcoming events.

- **Chicago Music Hotline,** 312-987-1123, opera and classical
- **Concert Line,** 312-666-6667, rock, country, blues
- **Dance Hotline,** 312-419-8383
- **Hot Tixx Hotline,** 312-977-1755, for a daily listing of shows offering discounted day-of-performance tickets either half price or $10 off. (Sunday tickets sold on Saturday.) The Hot Tixx offices are at 108 North State Street, 1616 Sherman Avenue in Evanston and at some Tower Records locations in the suburbs.
- **Theater Hotline,** 900-225-2225
- **TicketMaster** sells tickets to many Chicago cultural and sporting events by telephone. To order tickets by phone call 312-559-1212. There is a service charge added.

## ARCHITECTURE & NEIGHBORHOOD TOURS

No other city in the country is more well-known for its architecture, particularly its modern architecture. A walking tour of Chicago's buildings will open your eyes to the revolutionary and self-confident edifices erected in this most American of cities. Contact **The Chicago Architecture Foundation**, 224 South Michigan Avenue, 312-922-3432, for information.

If you're more of a people person, you might want to take a tour of one or more of Chicago's diverse and interesting neighborhoods. A tour is also a great way to learn about new parts of city in anticipation of a move. The city's Department of Cultural Affairs offers nine different **Chicago Neighborhood Tours** every Saturday. The four hour excursions leave from the Cultural Center at 77 East Randolph and cost $26 per person. Call 312-742-1190 for information.

## MUSIC

### CLASSICAL

The **Chicago Symphony Orchestra (CSO),** one of the most highly acclaimed orchestras in the world, plays at Orchestra Hall, 220 South Michigan Avenue, from September until June. For ticket information and sales, call 312-294-3000. In the summer, the CSO plays at **Ravinia Park** in north suburban Highland Park (Green Bay and Lake-Cook Roads), 847-266-5100, June through August.

The **Civic Orchestra of Chicago** is the training orchestra of the CSO. It plays six free concerts per year. Call Orchestra Hall, 312-294-3000, for ticket information.

The **Grant Park Symphony and Chorus** gives concerts all summer at the Petrillo Band Shell in Grant Park at Jackson Boulevard between Lake Shore Drive and Columbus Drive. You can purchase a reserved seat or listen for free on several acres of lawn. For information, call 312-742-4736. The city also sponsors separate blues, jazz, gospel and celtic festivals during the summer months as well as free ballroom dances with a live band; call the mayor's office at 312-744-4000 for more information.

Two smaller but no less entertaining orchestras are the **Chicago Chamber Orchestra**, 312-922-5570, and the **Chicago Sinfonietta**, 105 West Adams Street, 312-857-1062.

## OPERA

The **Lyric Opera of Chicago** performs at the Civic Center for the Performing Arts (commonly referred to as the Civic Opera House), 20 North Wacker Drive, from September through February. For information, call 312-332-2244.

## CHORUSES

Chicago has many singing companies that offer a wide range of musical genres at affordable prices.

- **Apollo Chorus of Chicago,** 630-960-2251
- **Halevi Choral Society,** 773-868-6700
- **The James Chorale,** 773-561-2424
- **Music of the Baroque,** 312-551-1415
- **The Oriana Singers,** 773-262-4558
- **Windy City Gay Chorus,** 773-404-9242

## BLUES

- **B.L.U.E.S., Etc.,** 1124 West Belmont Avenue, 773-525-8989
- **Blues Chicago** has two locations at 536 North Clark Street, 312-642-6261 and 736 North Clark Street, 312-661-0100.
- **Buddy Guy's Legends,** 754 South Wabash Avenue, 312-427-0333
- **Kingston Mines,** 2548 North Halsted Street, 773-477-4646
- **House of Blues,** 329 North Dearborn Street, 312-527-2583

## FOLK/COUNTRY

- **Abbey Pub and Restaurant,** 3420 West Grace Street, 773-478-4408
- **Old Town School of Folk Music,** 4544 N. Lincoln Avenue, 773-525-7793
- **Schubas,** 3159 North Southport Avenue, 773-525-2508

## JAZZ

- **Andy's Lounge,** 11 East Hubbard Street, 312-642-6805
- **Green Dolphin Street,** 2200 North Ashland Avenue, 773-395-0066

- **The Backroom**, 1007 North Rush Street, 312-751-2433
- **The Gold Star Sardine Bar**, 680 McClurg Court, 312-664-4215
- **The Green Mill**, 4802 North Broadway, 878-5552
- **Jazz Showcase**, 59 West Grand Avenue, 312-670-2473

## REGGAE

- **Culture Club**, 1351 South Michigan Avenue, 312-922-6414
- **Equator Club**, 4715 North Broadway, 773-728-2411
- **Exedus Lounge**, 3477 North Clark Street, 773-348-3998
- **Wild Hare, Ltd.**, 3530 North Clark Street, 773-327-4273

## ROCK/POP

- **Cubby Bear**, 1059 West Addison Street, 773-327-1642
- **Double Door**, 1572 North Milwaukee Avenue, 773-489-3160
- **Empty Bottle**, 1035 North Western Avenue, 773-276-3600
- **Liquid**, 1997 North Clybourn Avenue, 773-528-3400
- **The Metro**, 3730 North Clark Street, 773-549-0203
- **Park West**, 322 West Armitage Avenue, 773-929-5959
- **Riviera**, corner of Broadway and Lawrence Avenue, 773-275-6800

## NIGHTLIFE/DANCE CLUBS

If you're looking for a place to dance, see or be seen, try these places:

- **Buddha Lounge**, 728 West Grand Avenue, 312-266-2114
- **Dome Room**, 632 1/2 North Dearborn, 312-278-1009
- **Karma**, 318 West Grand Avenue, 312-321-1331
- **Red Dog**, 1958 West North, 773-278-1009
- **Shelter**, 564 West Fulton, 312-648-5500
- **Smart Bar**, 3730 North Clark, 773-549-4140
- **Stardust Cosmopolitan Lounge**, 440 North Halsted Street, 312-363-7827
- **The Note**, 1565 North Milwaukee Avenue, 773-489-0011
- **The Tunnel**, 809 West Evergreen, 312-751-8700

## DANCE

For upcoming dance events, call the **Dance Hotline**, 312-419-8383.

- **Ballet Chicago,** 312-251-8838
- **Columbia College Dance Center,** 773-989-3310
- **Gus Giordano Jazz Dance Chicago,** 847-866-9442
- **Hubbard Street Dance Company,** 312-663-0853
- **Joffrey Ballet of Chicago,** 312-739-0120

## THEATER

If you like theater, you've moved to the right city. Chicago is a great theater town, offering a spectrum from the large downtown halls to neighborhood storefronts. Many of the performing groups below offer season subscriptions. If you're on a severe budget and desperate to see some theater, you should know that many places, including the Steppenwolf, accept volunteer ushers. Simply call the box office to find out if they can use your services; after passing out programs you'll get a good house seat for free! See the *Reader's* weekly Theater Directory for a complete listing of the dozens of area theaters.

- **Bailiwick Repertory,** 1229 West Belmont Avenue, 773-883-1090
- **Body Politic/Victory Gardens,** 2257-61 North Lincoln Avenue, 773-871-3000
- **Briar Street Theatre,** 3133 North Halsted Street, 773-348-4000
- **Court Theatre,** 5535 South Ellis Avenue, 773-753-4472
- **Goodman Theatre,** 200 South Columbus Drive, 312-443-3800
- **Steppenwolf Theatre Company,** 1650 North Halsted Street, 312-335-1650
- **The Theatre Building,** 1225 West Belmont Avenue, 773-327-5252

In addition to these mostly North Side first-run theater companies, there are several large theaters in the Loop that offer Broadway previews and traveling shows. Chicago is also the home of the famed Second City and other improvisational and stand-up **comedy clubs.**

- **All Jokes Aside,** 1000 South Wabash Avenue, 312-922-0577
- **Improv Olympic,** 3541 North Clark Street, 773-880-0199
- **Second City Theatre,** 1616 North Wells Street, 312-337-3992
- **Zanies Comedy Club,** 1548 North Wells Street, 312-337-4027

# MUSEUMS

## ART MUSEUMS

- **The Art Institute of Chicago,** Michigan Avenue at Adams Street, 312-443-3600, is one of the finest art museums in the world. More than 4,000 years of art lie within its walls, as well as the best collection of French Impressionism outside the Musée d'Orsay. Admission charged (free on Tuesdays with later hours).
- **The Museum of Contemporary Art,** 220 East Chicago Avenue, 312-280-2660, specializes in postwar and contemporary art and keeps itself on the cutting edge. Free admission, first Tuesday of month.
- **Terra Museum of American Art,** 666 North Michigan Avenue, 312-664-3939, specializes in 18th-, 19th- and 20th-century American art. Late hours on Tuesday. Admission charged.
- **Museum of Contemporary Photography,** Columbia College, 600 South Michigan Avenue, 312-663-5554, is committed to promoting contemporary photography exclusively. Admission is free.

## MUSEUMS

- **The Adler Planetarium,** 1300 South Lake Shore Drive, 312-922-7827. The December "Star of Bethlehem" show (which offers an interesting explanation of the Christmas star) is not to be missed. Free admission to the museum; admission charged for the sky shows.
- **Chicago Architecture Foundation,** 224 South Michigan Avenue, 312-922-3432, offers tours of a city known world-wide for its architecture. Admission charged.
- **Chicago Children's Museum,** 700 East Grand Avenue (Navy Pier), 312-527-1000, is an incredible interactive space for the young and the young at heart. Admission charged (free on Thursday evenings, 5 p.m. - 8 p.m.).
- **Chicago Historical Society,** 1601 North Clark Street, 312-642-4600, is an excellent place to get to know the history of your new home. Admission charged.
- **DuSable Museum of African American History,** 740 East 56th Place, 773-947-0600, is named for Jean Baptiste Pointe DuSable, a black Haitian trader who was Chicago's first non-native settler. Admission charged (free on Thursdays).
- **Field Museum of Natural History,** Roosevelt Road at Lake Shore

Drive, 312-922-9410, has more than 19 million artifacts and where you go to see dinosaur bones in Chicago. Admission charged (free on Wednesdays).

- **International Museum of Surgical Science,** 1516 North Lake Shore Drive, 312-642-6502, presents the history of medicine; its many surgical instruments are not for the queasy. Admission is free.
- **Mexican Fine Arts Center Museum,** 1852 West 19th Street, 312-738-1503, the largest public collection of Mexican art and culture in the United States. Admission is free.
- **Museum of Broadcast Communication,** 78 East Washington Street, 312-629-6000, focuses on radio and television history; its archives have thousands of old radio and TV programs. Admission charged.
- **Museum of Science and Industry,** 57th Street and Lake Shore Drive, 773-684-1414, has hands-on exhibits that will fascinate young and old alike. Don't miss the Omnimax Theater. Admission charged (free day on Thursday).
- **The Newberry Library,** 60 West Walton Street, 312-943-9090, is not a museum, but it may as well be. It has a wide collection of rare books, maps and genealogical material. Admission is free.
- **Oriental Institute Museum,** 1155 East 58th Street, 773-702-9521, is the repository of many treasures of archaeological digs conducted through the decades by the University of Chicago. Admission is free.
- **Shedd Aquarium,** 1200 South Lake Shore Drive, 312-939-2438, brings the Seven Seas to Chicago, including beluga whales and porpoises in the new $43-million oceanarium. Admission charged (free on Thursdays).
- **Spertus Museum of Judaica,** 618 South Michigan Avenue, 312-922-9012, contains artifacts spanning centuries of Jewish history, tradition and culture. Admission charged.

## ART GALLERIES

Although not quite in the same league as New York's SoHo, Chicago has a gallery district of its own scattered roughly between Chicago and Grand Avenues on the "Lake" Streets (Superior, Huron, Erie). Generally, on the first Thursday or Friday of the month (call a gallery or look in the *Reader* to find out for sure) , galleries hold evening open houses, providing an opportunity to meet artists, see their work, and meet other art lovers. Below are just a few of the galleries:

- **Aldo Castillo Gallery,** 233 West Huron, 312-337-2536
- **Ann Nathan Gallery,** 218 West Superior, 312-664-9312
- **Carl Hammer Gallery,** 200 West Superior, 312-266-8512
- **Catherine Edelman Gallery,** 300 West Superior, 312-266-2350
- **Fassbender Gallery,** 309 West Superior, 312-951-5979
- **Oskar Friedl Gallery,** 750 North Orleans, 312-337-7550

## MOVIE THEATERS

The Chicago area, like the rest of the country, has been invaded by multi-plexes offering a dozen screens of the same commercial blockbuster. See the *Reader* for a complete screen directory. Here are some art, foreign and budget theaters that offer an alternative to the run of the mill box-office fare. Serious film buffs might also be interested in the annual **Chicago Film Festival** which is held for two weeks in early October. Call Cinema Chicago at 312-425-9400 for information.

- **Art Institute Film Center,** South Michigan Ave. and East Adams Street, 312-443-3737
- **Chicago Filmmakers,** 1543 West Division Street, 773-384-5533
- **Davis,** 4614 North Lincoln Avenue, 773-784-0893
- **Facets Multimedia Inc.,** 1517 West Fullerton Avenue, 773-281-4114
- **Fine Arts,** 418 South Michigan Avenue, 312-939-3700
- **Music Box,** 3733 North Southport Avenue, 773-871-6604
- **Piper's Alley,** 1608 North Wells Street, 312-642-7500
- **Three Penny,** 2424 North Lincoln Avenue, 773-935-5744
- **Village,** 1548 North Clark Street, 312-642-2403

WHEN THINKING OF CHICAGO, GREEN IS PROBABLY NOT THE first color that comes to mind; more than likely it's a smudgy, sooty, washed-out shade of gray. If the city's limited palette has got you down, if you're spending too much time staring down walls and sidewalks, it may be time for a visit to one of Chicago's parks or one of Cook County's forest preserves. A walk under the trees and through the grass will reopen your eyes to a sector of the color wheel you thought perhaps was gone forever.

## CHICAGO

The **Chicago Park District** (312-747-2200) is responsible for the upkeep of hundreds of parks throughout the city. These range in size from housing-lot-sized playgrounds to large, multi-use facilities like Lincoln and Jackson Parks. The obvious standout from all the rest is the system of lakeshore parks which stretches almost twenty miles from Ardmore Avenue (in the Edgewater neighborhood) to 67th Street (in South Shore). The lakeshore parks are Chicago's saving grace. The pressure of city living is somehow magically released in the presence of Lake Michigan. Chicago meets its match here. A city that was built on a swamp, that made its rivers run backwards, that completely changed the face of the land it grew on — is powerless to alter the lake. The crash of waves and the cries of gulls remind us of that fact.

Then again, most people probably head to the lakeshore for other reasons. Bikers, in-line skaters, walkers, and runners are there to get in shape. For those who like team sports, there are sports leagues and teams scattered throughout the park: volleyball on North Avenue Beach; baseball on the diamonds across from Waveland Avenue; soccer on the fields north of Montrose Avenue; rowers in the lagoon across from

Lincoln Park Zoo; sailors in Burnham Harbor; golfers at the 18 hole course in Jackson Park. Whatever you like to do, the lakeshore parks are the place to do it. Call the Park District (or look in the "Sports and Recreation" chapter) for more information.

If you want an even greener experience, visit **Lincoln Park Conservatory** (Fullerton Parkway and Stockton Drive, 312-742-7736) or **Garfield Park Conservatory** (300 North Central Park Avenue, 312-746-5100). Both have extensive permanent collections and offer spectacular flower shows throughout the year.

Another place to head for walks, and peace and quiet, are **Chicago's cemeteries**. Rosehill and Graceland are two of the larger, better-known cemeteries on the North Side. Here you will find the tombs and headstones of famous and not so famous Chicagoans. You will certainly recognize the names of Chicago streets, quite a few of which were named after people who were buried here.

## COOK COUNTY

The Forest Preserve District of Cook County maintains an extensive network of parks, forest preserves, walking and biking trails, golf courses, and fishing spots throughout the county. Call them at 800-870-3666 for brochures and information. The following are just some of the ways you could spend a day.

**Fishing:** there are over 35 lakes and ponds on which to wile away a lazy afternoon, but you will need a fishing license. The Forest Preserve District (FPD) puts out a brochure which contains the rules and regulations as well as detailed maps of each fishing area.

**Biking/Hiking/Walking:** they don't call them forest preserves for nothing. The FPD has over a hundred miles of trails which run through woods and sections of open grassland. The longest of these, the North Branch Bicycle Trail, runs from the northwest corner of Chicago to the Chicago Botanic Garden in Glencoe. It follows the North Branch of the Chicago River and is a weekend favorite for those who live in the suburbs adjacent to the trail. Individual brochures/maps are available for each trail.

**Nature Centers:** if you want a shorter hike but a more enlightening one, stop by one of the FPD's four nature centers. Frequent educational programs are offered throughout the year including bird walks, night walks, star gazing, maple syrup harvests, and all manner of things pertaining to nature and ecology.

**The Chicago Botanic Garden** (1000 Lake Cook Road, Glencoe,

60022, 847-835-5440) is a 385 acre oasis of plants and flowers divided into 21 separate gardens. Though not operated by the Forest Preserve District, it is located on District land. It is easily accessible from the Edens Expressway (I-94) or you can bike there on the North Branch Trail. If you are a plant lover, this is a definite must-see. There are rose gardens, re-creations of six different types of native prairies, and lovely water-lily ponds — Claude Monet would approve.

## SUBURBAN

Park District Numbers are:

- **Deerfield,** 847-945-0650
- **Des Plaines,** 847-391-5700
- **Evanston,** 847-866-2910
- **Northbrook,** 847-291-2960
- **Oak Park,** 708-383-0002
- **Rosemont,** 847-823-6685
- **Skokie,** 847-674-1500
- **Wilmette,** 847-256-6100

WHETHER YOU ARE A PARTICIPANT OR A FAN, CHICAGO IS A city that is sports crazy. In fact, if Chicago doesn't offer the sport you're looking for — whether to play or to watch — it probably doesn't exist. There's even a sport that is popular nowhere else in the United States — or the world — and that's 16-inch softball, a game that requires only a bat and a 16-inch Clincher softball.

## PROFESSIONAL SPORTS

### BASEBALL

Baseball season in Chicago begins in early April and lasts until the first week in October, unless the Cubs or White Sox find themselves in post-season play. Most new Chicagoans find themselves at Wrigley Field because they live on the North Side and have watched the Cubs on WGN (Channel 9), a cable TV "super station," but the sometime success of the White Sox has lured more than South Siders to the new Comiskey Park.

- **Chicago Cubs** (National League) Wrigley Field, 1060 West Addison Street, 60613, 773-404-2827, www.cubs.com. The Cubs sales department is happy to accommodate group outings of 20 persons or more. You can purchase Cubs tickets at the Wrigley Field box office, at Ticketmaster outlets (remember, they add a service charge) or by phone until two hours before game time with American Express, Discover, MasterCard or VISA cards by calling Ticketmaster at 312-831-CUBS or if you're out of state at 800-347-CUBS. Phone orders will be mailed or, if time does not permit mailing, held at the special Ticketmaster "will call" window.

  Note that only MasterCard, VISA and cash are accepted for ticket purchases at Wrigley Field.
- **Chicago White Sox** (American League) Comiskey Park, 333 West

35th Street, 60616, 312-674-1000 (TDD, hearing impaired service 312-451-5188). The White Sox sales department is happy to accommodate group outings of 20 persons or more. For the more budget-minded fan, all Monday night home contests are Family Night Half-Price games. You can purchase White Sox tickets at the Comiskey Park box office, at Ticketmaster outlets or by phone until three hours before game time with American Express, Discover, MasterCard or VISA cards by calling Ticketmaster at 312-831-1SOX. Phone orders will be mailed or, if time does not permit mailing, held at the special Ticketmaster "will call" window. There is a service charge added to the price of each ticket ordered by phone. Comiskey Park accepts all major credit cards.

## BASKETBALL

The professional basketball regular season begins in October, when baseball ends, and continues through April, with the NBA playoffs extending well into June. After winning five NBA championships in the last decade, a longer-than-normal season now seems likely in the Windy City, and the high-tech United Center is proving a fitting location for the team.

Chicago also has several Division I college basketball teams, including the DePaul Blue Demons, who play at the Rosemont Horizon; the Loyola Ramblers, who play at Loyola University; and the Northwestern Wildcats, who play at McGaw Hall.

- **Chicago Bulls** (National Basketball Association) United Center, 1901 West Madison Street, 60612; the corporate offices are located at 980 North Michigan Avenue, Chicago, IL 60611, 312-455-4000. These are the hottest tickets in town. Unless you're well connected, or willing to shell out big bucks to scalpers, your chances of finding last-minute tickets are slim. Tickets for individual games go on sale the last weekend of September at the United Center box office or through Ticketron. Group tickets go on sale through the Bulls front office in August. All groups must consist of 25 people, no more and no fewer, and are seated in the second balcony.

    You can purchase Bulls tickets at the United Center box office, at Ticketmaster outlets or by phone until three hours before game time with American Express, Discover, MasterCard or VISA cards by calling Ticketmaster at 312-559-1212. Phone orders will be held at a "will call" window. There is a service charge added to the price of each ticket ordered by phone. Good luck!

## FOOTBALL

The popularity of the Bears is evident by the approximately 60,000 die-hard Bears fans who, despite the team's less than stellar record, brave Chicago's notorious winter, a.k.a. "Bear weather," to attend home games at Soldier Field. Pre-season games start in August; the regular season ends in mid-December.

- **Chicago Bears** (National Football League) Ticket Information Office: 950 North Western, Lake Forest, 847-615-2327. Bears tickets are tough to find because most seats are held by season ticket holders. If you want to get on the waiting list to become a season ticketholder, good luck. There are about 9,000 people ahead of you. But don't give up hope. You can purchase Bears single game tickets by mail every year by sending a self-addressed stamped envelope to the Bears ticket information office in early May. The Bears return an order form, which you fill out and send back with a check on or after June 1. Any remaining tickets from the mail-order sale — and there aren't many — go to Ticketmaster for sale in July.

    You can purchase Bears tickets through Ticketmaster outlets or by phone with American Express, Discover, MasterCard or VISA cards by calling Ticketmaster at 312-559-1212. There is a service charge added to the price of each ticket ordered by phone.

## HOCKEY

Although not as high-profile as the Bears, Cubs and White Sox, the Chicago Blackhawks made it to the NHL Stanley Cup finals in 1992 — and lost. Like basketball, the regular NHL season runs from October until April with the Stanley Cup playoffs extending through the spring.

- **Chicago Blackhawks** (National Hockey League) United Center, 1901 West Madison Street, 60612, 312-455-7000. You can purchase Blackhawks tickets at the Stadium box office, at Ticketmaster outlets or by phone with American Express, Discover, MasterCard or VISA cards by calling Ticketmaster at 312-559-1212. There is a service charge added to the price of each ticket ordered by phone.
- **Chicago Wolves** (International Hockey League) Rosemont Horizon,

10550 Lunt Avenue, Rosemont, 60018, 847-390-0404 or 800-THE-WOLVES. A new team, the young, International Hockey League Wolves profited in 1994 from a NHL strike that brought them plenty of hockey-hungry fans. For individual tickets, call Ticketmaster at 312-559-1212 or stop by the Rosemont Horizon's box office at 6920 North Mannheim Road, 847-635-6601.

## SOCCER

Although the 1994 World Cup brought international fans to town for much of the summer, temporarily increasing the sport's visibility, in Chicago soccer has never quite caught on. First there was the outdoor Sting, then the indoor Power, now the city again has an outdoor team, the Major League expansion team, the Chicago Fire. They've just signed their first international star, Mexican goalie Jorge Campos and are ready to open their first season. Soccer season runs from early April through late September, with twenty home games.

- **Chicago Fire** (Major League Soccer) Offices: 311 West Superior Street, Suite 444, 60610, 888-657-3473 (888-MLS-FIRE) ; stadium: Soldier Field. For ticket information call the Fire's general information number at 888-MLS-FIRE. Order season passes or ticket packages from the League, using American Express, Discover, MasterCard or VISA. For individual tickets order by mail through the Chicago Fire Office (call first for pricing), or call Ticketmaster. Phone orders will be mailed or, if time does not permit mailing, held at the special Ticketmaster "will call" window. There is a service charge added to the price of each ticket.

## DRAG RACING

- **Raceway Track:** 130th and Ashland, 708-385-4035; the racing season runs April through October.

## PARTICIPANT SPORTS

# BICYCLING

The biking experience in Chicago is decidedly urban. With the exception of the spectacular lakeshore path, the rest of the city's designated bike routes are on city streets. If you plan on doing much biking, you should be prepared for inconsiderate — or, even worse, oblivious — motorists. That said, there are some good reasons why people choose to get around by bike.

Speed for one. During rush hour, you'll often get home faster on a bike than you will in a car. Whizzing by a quarter-mile long line of cars can be quite exhilarating. And you can forget about parking. You've got a guaranteed spot right outside your place of employment and it doesn't cost a dime. Last but not least, it's good for you; it may be work but it will definitely wind you down after a hard day at the office.

Some things to keep in mind. Get a good bike lock and use it properly. Chicago has a lot of bike thieves, and they are talented and committed. Buy a U-lock and make sure you lock your bike to a fixed object (the city has recently started installing bike racks, but parking meters work well). Look out for "dummy poles" which are regular street sign poles where the bolts holding the base to the pole have been removed; the thief merely lifts up the pole and your bike is gone. More importantly, make sure you lock *your frame* and *both your wheel rims* (if your wheels are of the quick-release variety) to the rack. Anything that isn't secured is fair game. Also, if you have a shiny, new bike (or a classy old one in mint condition) and you're afraid it may attract the attention of serious bike thieves, you have two options: using tape and/or some paint, try to "age" it's appearance or, if possible, don't lock it up outside at all; bring it in wherever you go (although this may be difficult). Finally, buy a good bike helmet — and use it!

As for specific routes, the lakefront path is almost 20 miles long and runs from the northern tip of Lincoln Park to south of Hyde Park. Bicycle rentals are available in stores and at various locations along the path. Take care, the paths can get very congested on summer afternoons and weekends with foot, in-line skate, and skateboard traffic. Inland from the lake, ride on the smaller north-south and east-west streets which run parallel to the busy main drags. Avoid the heavy traffic on Ashland Avenue, Western Avenue, Irving Park Road, and Sheridan Road north of Hollywood.

The **Chicagoland Bicycle Federation** publishes a seven-county map of government-designated off-road bicycle trails in the Chicago metropolitan area as well as bicyclist-recommended roads for cycling through the Chicago area. The map is available in most bike shops and at the Rand McNally Maps & Travel stores. For weekend riding, check out the bike trails in various Cook County Forest Preserves. Call 800-870-3666 for free maps and brochures.

Remember that on a bicycle you are subject to the same rules of the road as motor vehicles: You are expected to ride with traffic, not against it; signal your turns, do not weave in and out of traffic, and do not run red lights. In addition, it's an especially good idea to wear a helmet and bright reflective clothing when riding at night.

## BILLIARDS AND POOL

Just as Chicago has more bars and taverns per capita than any city in the United States, the ratio surely must extend to pool tables. (The film "The Color of Money" was shot in various pool halls around town.) Many new pool halls have opened after the recent growth of pool and billiards, but keep in mind that most bars in town will have a table or two in back. Here's a short list of places that are more billiards than booze:

- **The Corner Pocket,** has six tables, 2610 North Halsted Street, 773-281-0050.
- **The Cue Club,** has 10 tables, 2833 North Sheffield Avenue, 773-477-3661.
- **Stix,** has 21 tables, 3416 North Sheffield Avenue, 773-404-7849.
- **St. Paul Billiards,** has 13 tables, 1415 West Fullerton Avenue, 773-472-9494.

## BOATING

Lake Michigan is arguably Chicago's greatest asset. The Chicago Park District and several lakefront yacht clubs offer sailing lessons and sailboat rental during the summer.

For sailing lessons, try the **Chicago Sailing Club** at Belmont Harbor, 773-871-7245, or **Fairwind Sail Charters**, Burnham Harbor, 312-427-1525. The **Chicago Park District** also offers sailing lessons, but classes fill in the spring. Call the Park District at 312-747-0737 for more information. **American Youth Hostels** also offers lessons - call 773-327-8114 for dates and prices.

If you own a boat and want to dock it in any of Chicago's harbors, you must lease a space through the Chicago Park District. There is a long waiting list for docking space.

## BOWLING

If you placed Chicago's bowling alleys end to end, they would circle the globe. Actually, this may not be true, but it sure seems like it. There are bowling alleys in nearly every neighborhood and many that sponsor leagues. With so many bowling alleys from which to choose, here are a few recommendations:

- **Diversey/River Bowl** has 36 lanes, 2211 West Diversey Avenue, 773-227-5800 They feature a Saturday night Rock-n-Bowl. Patrons bowl to rock music blasted through the public address system until 2:30 a.m. Open 24 hours on weekends.
- **Marigold Arcade** has 32 lanes, 828 West Grace Street, 773-935-8183. Marigold has a junior bowling program for ages 8 to 18.
- **North Center Bowl & Billiards** has 12 lanes, 4017 North Lincoln Avenue, 773-549-2360. The entrance of North Center is tough to find. Look for the door under the Old Style sign and go up the stairs.
- **Southport Lanes & Billiards** has four lanes, 3325 North Southport Avenue, 773-472-1601. If you see a pair of legs standing where you've just hurled your bowling ball, you're not drunk. Southport Lanes, a 75 year old institution, is the last bowling alley in Chicago to use human rather than automatic pinsetters.
- **Spencer's Marina City Bowl** has 38 lanes, 300 North State Street, 312-527-0747. If you're looking for a place to unwind after work, Marina City Bowl is perfect, conveniently located in the Marina City complex (the building behind the towers).
- **Waveland Bowl, Inc.** has 40 lanes, 3700 North Western Avenue, 773-472-5900. For those who need to kegel at 3 a.m. in the middle of the week, Waveland Bowl is the place for you. Open 24 hours a day, seven days a week.

## CASINO GAMBLING

Though not a sport to most, casino gambling is certainly a serious form of entertainment to many. If the lottery isn't enough for you, you don't have to go to go to Wisconsin or Las Vegas anymore; now there's "riverboat gambling" on the scenic Des Plaines river 15 miles south of Chicago in

Joliet. Also, just over the state line, Indiana offers "lake boat gambling" on Lake Michigan.

- **Empress Casino**, 888-436-7737, in Joliet and Hammond, liquor served, no entertainment.
- **Harrah's**, 800-427-7247, in Joliet, liquor served, entertaiment/ music.
- **Trump Casino**, 888-218-7867, Buffington Harbor, Indiana, liquor served, no entertainment.

## GOLF

The Chicago metropolitan area has miles of fairways for your golfing pleasure. The **Chicago Park District** runs six courses: Robert A. Black (9 holes, 2045 West Pratt Avenue), Columbus Park (9 holes, 5200 West Jackson Boulevard), Jackson Park (18 holes, 63rd and Stoney Island), Sydney A. Marovitz née Waveland (9 holes, 3600 North at the Lakefront; exit Lake Shore Drive at Addison or Irving Park), Marquette Park (9 holes, Marquette Road and Kedzie Avenue), and South Shore Country Club (9 holes, 71st Street and South Shore Drive).

To make reservations or for more information call the Park District at 312-245-0909. In addition to golf courses, the Chicago Park District also has driving ranges in Lincoln Park at Diversey and at its Jackson Park and Robert A. Black courses.

The **Cook County Forest Preserve** also runs a number of golf courses. They include Billy Caldwell (9 holes, 6200 North Caldwell Avenue, Chicago, 773-792-1930), "Chick" Evans (18 holes, 6145 Golf Road, Morton Grove, 847-965-5353), Edgebrook (18 holes, 5900 North Central Avenue, Chicago, 773-763-8320), and Indian Boundary (18 holes, 8600 West Forest Preserve Drive, Chicago, 773-625-9630).

Dozens of public and private golf courses dot the suburbs. Some of the more popular courses include:

**North:** Bonnie Brook Golf Course (18 holes, 2800 North Lewis Avenue, Waukegan, 847-336-5538), Glenview Park (18 holes, 800 Shermer Road, Glenview, 847-724-0250), Marriott's Lincolnshire Resort (18 holes, 10 Marriott Drive, Lincolnshire, 847-634-5935), Midlane Country Club (18 holes, 4555 West York House Road, Wadsworth, 847-244-1990), Pine Meadow (18 holes, Butterfield Road and Lake Street, Mundelein, 847-566-4653), Sportsman Country Club (27 holes, 3535

Dundee Road, Northbrook, 847-291-2350)

**Northwest:** Arlington Lakes (18 holes, 1211 South New Wilke Road, Arlington Heights, 847-577-3030), Chevy Chase (18 holes, 1000 North Milwaukee Avenue, Wheeling, 847-537-0082), Golf Club of Illinois (18 holes, 1575 Edgewood Road, Algonquin, 847-658-4400), Kemper Lakes, Old McHenry Road, Hawthorn Woods, 847-320-3450), Old Orchard Country Club (18 holes, 700 West Rand Road, Mt. Prospect, 847-255-2025), Villa Olivia Country Club (18 holes, U.S. Highway 20 and Naperville Road, Bartlett, 630-289-5200), Wilmette (18 holes, 3900 Fairway Drive, Wilmette, 847-256-9777)

**West:** Cantigny Golf (27 holes, 27 West 270 Mack Road, Wheaton, 630-668-3323), Indian Lakes Resort (36 holes, 250 West Schick Road, Bloomingdale, 630-529-6466)

**South and Southwest:** Carriage Greens (18 holes, 8700 Carriage Greens Drive, Darien, 630-985-3730), Cog Hill (72 holes, including the infamous Dubsdread, 119th Street and Archer Avenue, Lemont, 630-257-5872), Evergreen Country Club, (18 holes, 9100 South Western Avenue, 773-238-6680), Gleneagles Country Club (36 holes, 123rd Street and Bell Road, Lemont, 630-257-5466), Hickory Hills Country Club (27 holes, 8201 West 95th Street, Hickory Hills, 708-598-6460), Silver Lakes (45 holes, 147th Street and 82nd Avenue, Orland Park, 630-349-6944)

## HORSEBACK RIDING

Believe it or not, there is a place in Chicago where you can not only ride a horse, but you can board one and take riding lessons as well. The **Noble Horse Equestrian Center,** 1410 North Orleans Street, 312-266-7878, is the last riding center in the city of Chicago. It has a 200-foot by 75-foot indoor riding arena and space to board more than 60 horses. Riding lessons, dressage, jumping and hunt seat lessons also are available. Group lessons begin at $24 per hour; private lessons start at $25 per half hour.

In addition to the Noble Center, there are many stables in the northwest and southwest suburbs which offer everything from equestrian to trail riding for riders of all ages and skill levels. Check the Yellow Pages under "Stables."

## HORSE RACING

Prefer to play the ponies rather than ride them? There are four racetracks in the Chicago area:

- **Balmoral Park Racetrack,** Rt. 394 & Calumet Expressway, Crete, IL, 708-672-7544 harness racing year-round.
- **Hawthorne Race Course,** 3501 South Laramie Avenue, Cicero, IL, 708-780-3700; thoroughbred racing starts in October and runs through December. Harness racing is held in January.
- **Maywood Park Race Track,** 8600 West North Avenue, Maywood, IL, 708-343-4800; harness racing February through May.
- **Sportsman's Park,** 3301 South Laramie Avenue, Cicero, IL, 773-242-1121; thoroughbred racing starts in February and runs into May. Harness racing runs from May until October.

In case you can't make it to the tracks, there are two off-track betting parlors in the Loop at 177 North State Street (312-419-8787) and 233 West Jackson Boulevard (312-427-2300).

More information on Illinois racetracks and racing schedules can be found at the **Illinois Racing Board,** 100 West Randolph Street, 312-814-2600.

## IN-LINE SKATING AND ICE SKATING

During the summer, in-line skaters abound on the lakefront, so many in fact that it can be hazardous for pedestrians. If you want to participate, there are roller-blade rental shacks dotting the lakefront and Lincoln Park. Both of these retail outlets rent in-line skates.

- **Rainbo Sports Shop,** 4836 North Clark Street, 773-275-5500
- **Londo Mondo Motionwear,** 1100 North Dearborn Street, 312-751-2794

If ice is your element, Chicago has skating rinks in many parks throughout the city. Downtown, try "Skate on State" and the Daley Bicentennial Plaza at the north end of Grant Park.

## RUGBY

Chicago has rugby clubs for both men and women. The season runs from late March until late May and then again in the autumn from Labor Day into November. If having your brains beaten out on the field and then drinking your brains out with your erstwhile opponents sounds like your kind of fun, call:

- **Chicago Griffins Rugby Football Club Inc.,** 773-588-0350
- **Lincoln Park Rugby Football Club,** 773-528-8844

## RUNNING

Chicago's lakefront provides an ideal place for running all year round, although newcomers are advised to prepare for the winter wind off the lake. In the summer, be advised that you'll be competing with bikers and roller bladers in addition to the usual lakefront crowds. There are competitive races throughout the year, and some parks hold weekly events. Check the *Sun-Times* or *Tribune* for schedules. It goes without saying that you should avoid running after dark in areas where there are few people.

If you're really serious about running, check out the **Chicago Area Runners Association,** 203 North Wabash Avenue, 312-666-9836. CARA is the largest association of runners in the Midwest. It organizes races and training runs and acts as a lobbyist for runners' rights. The association successfully lobbied a lakefront alderman to keep the Lincoln Park running paths plowed through the winter.

The Chicago Marathon is held every year on the last Sunday in October. A world-class field as well as 10,000 other runners participate.

## SOFTBALL

There are hundreds of teams — 16-inch, 12-inch fast and 12-inch slow-pitch — playing in leagues across the Chicago area. Most teams are sponsored by employers, bars and restaurants. To get involved, keep an eye open and ask around. It shouldn't take too long to find someone who has a line on a team. You can also call the individual parks for information. Call the Chicago Park District at 312-747-2200 for information on the park and league nearest you.

## SOCCER

As a city with strong Latin American roots, Chicago always has been a soccer playing town.

If you're looking to join a team, contact the **Illinois Soccer Association,** 5306 West Lawrence, 773-283-2800, for information about outdoor and indoor leagues. The outdoor season starts in April and runs through September; indoor leagues run from autumn to spring.

## SWIMMING

Despite its easy access, Lake Michigan might not be the place you want to take your swim. The problem is not pollution but temperature. The lake can be too cold for swimming for all but the hardiest individuals until well into the summer. For those who prefer the lake to pool laps, many long-distance swimmers will swim parallel to the shoreline from Ohio Street to the Oak Street curve and from Oak Street Beach to North Avenue pier.

The Chicago Park District has outdoor pools throughout the city, but these are usually filled with screaming kids enjoying summer vacation. Check to see if the pools have special times for adult swims.

The Park District's indoor pools are one of Chicago's best-kept secrets. They are free, well-maintained, and there are more than 30 scattered throughout the city. They lack the luxury and amenities of health clubs and private pools, but they'll get you in shape just as quickly. If you're interested, call the Park District at 312-747-2200 for the pool nearest you, or look in the White Pages under "Chicago Park District." Hours, frequency, and duration of lap swims vary from facility to facility, so call ahead.

Here are two you might want to check out. **Welles Park** (2333 West Sunnyside Avenue, 312-742-7515) in the Lincoln Square neighborhood is a full-sized pool in a beautiful building with many windows and lots of natural light. **Gill Park** (825 West Sheridan Road, 312-742-7802) in Wrigleyville is the place for serious swimmers. There are lap swims three times a day and the pace can be blistering; if you're a novice, you'll want to stay in the slow lane.

Health clubs and YMCAs throughout the city also have pools for the serious swimmer. Many high-rise apartment buildings have their own pools, but these are more for quick dips while sunning on a nearby chaise lounge than a serious workout.

Private swimming pool clubs include the **McClurg Court Sports Center** (333 East Ontario Street, 312-944-4546), and the **South Plymouth Court Swimming Pool Association** (1151 South Plymouth Court, 312-427-4950).

## TENNIS

The Chicago Park District has nearly 700 tennis courts in parks throughout the city, but be warned: the good ones are packed and the bad ones look like the surface of the moon. The best Park District tennis courts are in Lincoln Park between Addison Street and Irving Park Road and at the south end of Grant Park east of Columbus Drive.

There are also courts at some private health clubs, including the

Lakeshore Athletic Club, 1320 West Fullerton Avenue, 773-477-9888, and the Mid-Town Tennis Club, 2020 West Fullerton Avenue, 773-235-2300.

## HEALTH CLUBS

Staying fit is not an easy job, but somebody has to do it. Fortunately, Chicago has an abundance of health clubs and workout centers ranging from little more than weight and machine rooms to extensive clubs that offer aerobics, tennis courts, swimming pools and indoor jogging tracks. Keep in mind that although you can get a workout at almost every club, a few are places where members go to "see and be seen" as well as exercise. A word of advice: take a tour or ask if you can work out once for free to really "try" it out before you take the plunge.

- **ACIC Club,** 211 North Stetson Avenue, 312-616-9000; in addition to the usual amenities, the club offers a climbing wall for rock-climbing enthusiasts.
- **Bally's Chicago Total Fitness** centers are located throughout Chicago. Downtown locations are 25 East Washington Street, 312-372-7755; 230 West Monroe Street, 312-263-4500; and 800 South Wells Street, 312-431-0100. There also is a club at 2828 North Clark Street, 773-929-6900. The pulsating TV commercials notwithstanding, quality of service and equipment at Bally's varies considerably. Tour/try the place before splurging and regretting. For general information call 800-695-8111.
- **Chicago Athletic Association,** 12 South Michigan Avenue, 312-236-7500; the address says it all, and the dress code too (no jeans). As much social club as health club, the CAA has been around for over a century.
- **Combined Fitness Centre,** 1235 North LaSalle Street, 312-787-8400
  **East Bank Club,** 500 North Kingsbury Street, 312-527-5800. Three blocks long, this monument to fitness claims to be the largest health club in the United States.
  **Hyde Park Athletic Club,** 1301 East 47th Street, 773-548-1300
  **Lakeshore Athletic Club,** 441 North Wabash Avenue, 312-644-4880; 1320 West Fullerton Avenue, 773-477-9888
  **Lehmann Sports Club,** 2700 North Lehmann Court, 773-871-8300
  **McClurg Court Sports Center,** 333 East Ontario Street, 312-944-4546

- **Onterie Fitness Center,** 446 East Ontario Street, 312-642-0031
- **Presidential Fitness,** Northbrook, 707 Skokie Boulevard, 847-272-8910
- **River North Fitness,** 820 North Orleans Avenue, 312-664-6537
- **Webster Fitness Club,** 957 West Webster Avenue, 773-248-2006
- **Women's Workout World** has five locations: 1031 North Clark Street, 312-664-2106; 2540 West Lawrence Avenue, 773-334-7341; 3125 North Knox Avenue, 773-725-3055; 5201 South Harper Avenue, 773-684-3000; and 5030 South Kedzie Avenue, 773-434-8900.

Chicago **YMCAs** are a good place if you're looking for a no-frills health club. Many Ys have all of the amenities of the popular health clubs at a fraction of the cost. You can call the YMCA of Metropolitan Chicago, 312-280-3400, for the Y nearest you. Two of the more popular Ys are the **New City YMCA,** 1515 North Halsted Street, 312-266-1242, and the **Lincoln-Belmont YMCA,** 3333 North Marshfield Avenue, 773-248-3333.

Finally, you might want to call your local **hospital** and see if they have a fitness center. An increasing number of hospitals operate non-profit fitness centers both as preventive/rehabilitative medicine and as a marketing tool. These hospital gyms can be mellower than the commercial gyms and the dues correspondingly reasonable.

For a monthly guide to upcoming sporting events and sports-related articles pick up a copy of *Windy City Sports* (312-421-1551). It's available free of charge at local sporting goods stores and bike shops. Finally, if you like to participate in organized sports and want to make friends at the same time, consider joining the sports oriented **Chicago Social Club,** 773-883-9596. Leagues are running year-round in different sports depending upon the season: In winter, there's indoor volleyball; in spring, indoor volleyball and touch football; in summer, beach volleyball and softball; in fall, touch football and basketball.

C HICAGO, WITH ITS HUNDREDS OF THOUSANDS OF IRISH, POLISH, and most recently, Hispanic immigrants, is still a predominantly Roman Catholic city. Today there are about 2,300,000 Roman Catholics in the Archdiocese of Chicago. Although they don't cut as high a profile, Protestant churches and Jewish synagogues thrive in almost every neighborhood as well, and you're likely to find one near you.

Choosing a place of worship is a personal decision. The list in this guide doesn't pretend to be complete, but it's a place to start until you get more familiar with Chicago. If you want the full list of houses of worship in Chicago, check the Yellow Pages under "Churches," "Synagogues," and "Religious Organizations."

## CHURCHES

### ROMAN CATHOLIC

(Call the Archdiocese of Chicago, 312-751-8200, for information on Cook and Lake counties.)

- **Holy Name Cathedral,** 735 North State Street, 312-787-8040, is the see of the Archdiocese of Chicago.
- **Nativity of Our Lord,** 653 West 37th Street, 773-927-6263
- **Old St. Mary's,** 23 East Van Buren Street, 312-922-3444
- **Old St. Patrick's,** 700 West Adams Street, 312-782-6171, was founded by Irish immigrants, and is the oldest church in Chicago.
- **Our Lady of Lourdes,** 4640 North Ashland Avenue, 773-561-2141
- **Our Lady of Mount Carmel,** 690 West Belmont Avenue, 773-525-0453
- **Queen of Angels,** 2330 West Sunnyside Avenue, 773-561-5118
- **St. Alphonsus Redemptorist,** 1429 West Wellington Street, 773-525-0709
- **St. Andrew,** 3546 North Paulina Street, 773-525-3016
- **St. Barnabas,** 10134 South Longwood Drive, 773-779-1166

- **St. Benedict's,** 2215 West Irving Park Road, 773-588-6484
- **St. Clement's,** 642 West Deming Place, 773-281-0371
- **St. Francis of Assisi,** 817 West Roosevelt Road, 312-850-1448
- **St. Hedwig,** 2226 North Hoyne Avenue, 773-486-1660
- **St. Ita's,** 5500 North Broadway, 773-561-5343
- **St. John Cantius,** 825 North Carpenter Street, 312-243-7373, is one of the few churches in Chicago that has a Latin mass.
- **St. Josaphat,** 2311 North Southport Avenue, 773-327-8955
- **St. Margaret Mary,** 2324 West Chase Avenue, 773-764-0615
- **St. Mary of the Angels,** 1850 North Hermitage Avenue, 773-278-2644
- **St. Mary of the Lake,** 4200 North Sheridan Road, 773-472-3711
- **St. Michael's,** 1633 North Cleveland Avenue, 312-642-2498
- **St. Nicholas Ukrainian Catholic Cathedral,** 2238 West Rice Street, 773-276-4537
- **St. Peter's,** 110 West Madison Street, 312-372-5111
- **St. Stanilaus Kostka,** 1351 West Evergreen Avenue, 773-278-2470
- **St. Stephen King of Hungary,** 2015 West Augusta Boulevard, 773-486-1896
- **St. Teresa's,** 1037 West Armitage Avenue, 773-528-6650
- **St. Thomas the Apostle,** 5472 South Kimbark Avenue, 773-324-2626
- **St. Vincent de Paul,** 1010 West Webster Avenue, 773-327-1113

## EASTERN ORTHODOX

- **Holy Nativity Romanian Church,** 6350 North Paulina Street, 773-743-9648
- **Holy Trinity Cathedral Orthodox Church,** 1121 North Leavitt Street, 773-486-4545
- **St. George Orthodox Cathedral,** 917 North Wood Street, 312-666-5179

## BAPTIST

- **North Shore Baptist Church,** 5244 North Lakewood Avenue, 773-728-4200
- **Uptown Baptist Church,** 1011 West Wilson Avenue, 773-784-2922

## CHRISTIAN SCIENCE

- **Second Church of Christ Scientist,** 2700 North Pine Grove Avenue, 773-549-3362

- **Sixteenth Church of Christ Scientist,** 7036 North Ridge Avenue, 773-764-0300
- **Seventeenth Church of Christ Scientist,** 55 East Wacker Drive, 312-236-4671

## EPISCOPAL

- **All Saints Church,** 4550 North Hermitage Avenue, 773-61-0111
- **Brent House,** 5540 South Woodlawn Avenue, 773-947-8744
- **Church of the Ascension,** 1133 North LaSalle Street, 312-664-1271
- **Church of Our Savior,** 530 West Fullerton Avenue, 773-549-3832
- **St. Chrysostom's,** 1424 North Dearborn Parkway, 312-944-1083
- **St. James Cathedral,** 65 East Huron Street, 312-787-7360, is Chicago's oldest Episcopal church.

## LUTHERAN/EVANGELICAL

- **Augustana Lutheran Church of Hyde Park,** 5500 South Woodlawn Avenue, 773-493-6451
- **Ebenezer Lutheran Church,** 1650 West Foster Avenue, 773-561-8496
- **Holy Trinity Lutheran Church,** 1218 West Addison Street, 773-248-1233
- **Lake View Lutheran Church,** 835 West Addison Street, 773-327-1427
- **Metropolitan Chicago Synod,** 18 South Michigan Avenue, 312-346-3150
- **Resurrection Lutheran Church,** 3303 North Seminary Avenue, 773-525-0605
- **Rogers Park Lutheran Church,** 1701 West Morse Avenue, 773-764-6075
- **Wicker Park Lutheran Church,** 2112 West LeMoyne Street, 773-276-0263

## LUTHERAN/MISSOURI SYNOD

- **Bethany Evangelical Lutheran Church,** 1244 West Thorndale Avenue, 773-561-9159
- **First St. Paul's Evangelical Lutheran Church,** 1301 North LaSalle Street, 312-642-7172
- **St. James Evangelical Lutheran Church,** 2046 North Fremont Street, 773-549-1615

## METHODIST

- **Chicago Methodist Temple,** 77 West Washington Street, 312-236-4548; This First United Methodist Church of Chicago is the oldest congregation in Chicago, dating to 1831, before the city's incorporation.

## PRESBYTERIAN

- **Second Presbyterian Church,** 1936 South Michigan Avenue, 312-225-4951
- **Fourth Presbyterian Church,** 126 East Chestnut Street, 312-787-4570
- **Lake View Presby Church,** 716 West Addison Street, 773-281-2655
- **Lincoln Park Presbyterian Church,** 600 West Fullerton Parkway, 773-248-8288
- **Rogers Park Presbyterian Church,** 7059 North Greenview Avenue, 773-262-3667

## NON-DENOMINATIONAL

- **Moody Church,** 1609 North LaSalle Drive, 312-943-0466
- **Rockefeller Memorial Chapel,** 5850 South Woodlawn Avenue, 773-702-2100

## UNITARIAN

- **First Unitarian Church,** 5650 South Woodlawn Avenue, 773-324-4100.
- **Unitarian Unity Temple,** 875 Lake Street, Oak Park, 708-848-6225; designed by Frank Lloyd Wright.

## UNITED CHURCH OF CHRIST

- **St. Paul's United Church of Christ,** 2335 North Orchard Street, 773-348-3829
- **University Church,** 5655 South University Avenue, 773-363-8142
- **Wellington Avenue United Church of Christ,** 615 West Wellington Avenue, 773-935-0642

# SYNAGOGUES

## RECONSTRUCTIONIST

- **Jewish Reconstructionist Congregation**, 303 Dodge Avenue, Evanston, 847-328-7678

## REFORM

- **Chicago Sinai Congregation**, 1 East Delaware Place, 312-867-7000
- **Congregation Kol Ami**, 845 North Michigan Avenue, 312-664-4775
- **Emanuel Congregation**, 5959 North Sheridan Road, 773-561-5173
- **KAM Isaiah Israel Congregation**, 1100 East Hyde Park Boulevard, 773-924-1234
- **North Shore Congregation Israel**, 1185 Sheridan Road, Glencoe, 847-835-0724
- **Oak Park Temple**, 1235 North Harlem Avenue, Oak Park, 708-386-3937
- **Temple Sholom**, 3480 North Lake Shore Drive, 773-525-4707
- **University of Chicago Hillel**, 5715 South Woodlawn, 773-752-1127; (focus is university community - limited events open to public).

## CONSERVATIVE

- **Anshe Emet Synagogue**, 3760 North Pine Grove Avenue, 773-281-1423; is the oldest synagogue in Chicago.
- **Central Synagogue of the Southside Hebrew Congregation**, 150 East Huron Street, 312-787-0450
- **Congregation Ezra-Habonim**, 2620 West Touhy Avenue, 773-743-0154
- **Congregation Kol Emeth**, 5130 Touhy Avenue, Skokie, 847-673-3370
- **Congregation Rodfei Zedek**, 5200 South Hyde Park Boulevard, 773-752-2770
- **Niles Township Jewish Congregation**, 4500 West Dempster Street, Skokie, from Chicago 773-583-2191
- **North Sheridan Hebrew Congregation**, 6301 North Sheridan Road, 773-262-0330
- **University of Chicago Hillel**, 5715 South Woodlawn, 773-752-1127; (focus is university community - limited events open to public).

## ORTHODOX

For information: **Chicago Rabbinical Council,** 773-588-1600
- **Anshe Sholom B'nai Israel Congregation,** 540 West Melrose Street, 773-248-9200
- **Chicago Loop Synagogue,** 16 South Clark Street, 3312-46-7370
- **Congregation Beth Itzchok of West Rogers Park,** 6716 North Whipple Street, 773-973-2522
- **Lubavitch Chabad of Lincoln Park,** 515 West Grant Place, 773-281-7770
- **University of Chicago Hillel,** 5715 South Woodlawn, 773-752-1127; (focus is university community - limited events open to public).

### ISLAM

- **The Islamic Center of Chicago,** 4033 North Damen Avenue, 773-477-0003
- **The Muslim Community Center,** 4380 North Elston Avenue, 773-725-9047
- **The Nation of Islam,** 734 West 79th, 773-602-1230

### OTHER

- **Baha'i House of Worship,** 100 Linden Avenue, Wilmette, 847-853-2300
- **Midwest Buddhist Temple,** 435 West Menomonee Street, 312-943-7801

I F, AFTER HAVING SETTLED IN, YOU FIND YOURSELF WITH SOME FREE time and want to make Chicago and the world a better place, there are plenty of opportunities in the city for you to volunteer your services or join an advocacy group.

Pick your cause — from Big Brother/Big Sister programs to assisting with voter registration — and make some phone calls. Any organization will be happy to hear from you. Your involvement can give you personal satisfaction and perhaps a whole new circle of friends.

If you don't know where to start, a good place to call is The **Volunteer Center of the United Way/Crusade of Mercy**, 312-906-2245. They will be more than happy to steer you to a not-for-profit group that best suits your interests. The **Association House of Chicago**, 773-276-0084, also provides a variety of community services that cross age and cultural barriers. Or, when visiting your local bookstore or library, pick up a free copy of *ICARE*, a guide to Chicagoland charities and non-profit organizations.

## AIDS

- AIDS Action Line, 800-243-2437
- AIDS Research Alliance: Chicago, 773-244-5800
- Better Existence with HIV (BEHIV), 847-475-2115
- Bonaventure House, Inc., 773-327-9921
- Chicago House and Social Service Agency, 773-248-5200
- The Children's Place Association, 773-826-1230

## ALCOHOL

- Alcoholics Anonymous, 312-346-1475
- Alliance Against Intoxicated Motorists (AAIM), 847-697-2246
- Mothers Against Drunk Driving (MADD), 312-782-6266

## CANCER

- American Cancer Society, National, 312-641-6150
- American Cancer Society, Chicago North Area, 773-792-3300, or 1-800-227-2345

## CHILDREN

- Big Brothers/Big Sisters of Metropolitan Chicago, 312-427-0637
- Boy Scouts of America, Chicago Area Council, 312-421-8800
- Boys & Girls Clubs of Chicago, 312-627-2700
- Girl Scouts of Chicago, 312-416-2500

## COMMUNITY SERVICES

- Ada S. McKinley Community Services, 312-554-2313
- Jane Addams Hull House Association, 312-906-8600

## CRIME PREVENTION

- Chicago Crime Commission, 773-372-0101
- Illinois Council Against Handgun Violence, 312-341-0939

## EDUCATION

- Cabrini-Green Tutoring Program, 312-467-4980
- Midtown Educational Foundation, 312-738-8300
- Tuesday's Child (parent training program), 773-248-6394

## ENVIRONMENT

- Center for Neighborhood Technology, 773-278-4800, ext.127
- Citizens for a Better Environment, 312-939-1530
- Friends of the Park, 312-922-3307
- Greenpeace USA, Inc., 312-563-6060
- Lake Michigan Federation, 312-939-0838
- Nature Conservancy, 312-346-8166
- North Branch Prairie Restoration Project, 773-878-3877
- Open Lands Project, 312-427-4256
- Sierra Club, 312-251-1680

# FOSTER CARE/ADOPTION

- Jewish Children's Bureau of Chicago, 312-444-2090
- Lawrence Hall Youth Services, 773-769-3500
- Volunteers of America - Illinois, 312-707-8707

# GAY AND LESBIAN

- Gay & Lesbian Anti-Violence Project, 773-871-2273
- Horizons Community Services, 773-472-6469
- Howard Brown Health Center, 773-871-5777
- Parents and Friends of Lesbians and Gays (PFLAG), 773-472-3079

# HEALTH/DISEASE

- American Diabetes Association, 312-346-1805
- American Heart Association of Metro Chicago, 312-346-4675
- American Red Cross, Mid-America Chapter, 312-440-2000
- Epilepsy Foundation of Greater Chicago, 312-939-8622
- Juvenile Diabetes Foundation, 312-670-0313
- Les Turner ALS Foundation (Lou Gehrig's disease), 847-679-3311
- Leukemia Research Foundation, 847-982-1480
- Leukemia Society of America, 312-726-0003
- Make a Wish Foundation of Northern Illinois, 312-943-8956
- National Kidney Foundation of Illinois, 312-663-3103
- United Cerebral Palsy of Greater Chicago, 312-368-0380

# HISTORICAL/RESTORATION

- Chicago Historical Society, 312-642-4600
- Rogers Park/West Ridge Historical Society, 773-764-4078
- Skokie Historical Society, 847-673-1888

# HOMELESS/FOOD

- Care for Real, 773-769-6182
- Chicago Coalition for the Homeless, 312-435-4548
- Community Emergency Shelter Organization (CESO), 312-913-2040
- Crusaders of America, 773-275-5949
- Greater Chicago Food Depository, 773-247-3663

- Habitat for Humanity, Midwest Region, 312-243-6448
- Inspiration Care, 773-878-0981
- Lakeview Pantry, 773-525-1777
- Pacific Garden Mission, 312-922-1462
- Voice of the People Uptown, Inc. (VOP), 773-769-2442

## LEGAL

- American Civil Liberties Union, 312-201-9740
- Chicago Lawyers Committee for Civil Rights Under Law, Inc., 312-630-9744
- Lawyers for the Creative Arts, 312-944-2787
- Legal Assistance Foundation of Chicago, 312-949-5390

## LITERACY

- Illinois Adult Learning Hotline, 800-321-9511
- Literacy Volunteers of Chicago, 312-236-0341
- Reading Is Fundamental, 312-507-3947

## PEOPLE WITH DISABILITIES

- Access Living of Metropolitan Chicago, 312-226-5900; TDD, 312-226-1687
- A Gift from the Heart Foundation, 773-777-2306
- America's Disabled Children, Inc., 773-685-7111
- Association for Retarded Citizens of Illinois, 708-206-1930
- Blind Service Association Inc., 312-236-0808
- Chicago Association for Retarded Citizens, 312-346-6230
- Chicago Lighthouse for the Blind, 312-666-1331
- Contact Chicago, 773-728-0780
- Guild for the Blind, 312-236-8569
- Illinois Society for the Prevention of Blindness, 312-922-8710
- Illinois Special Olympics, 312-595-9138
- Lester and Rosalie Anixter Center, 773-273-1000
- Misericordia Home, 773-973-6300
- Sunshine Activity Center, 773-283-0089

## POLITICS

- Amnesty International, 312-427-2060
- Better Government Association, 312-641-1181
- Chicago Voter Registration Coalition, 312-427-6220
- League of Women Voters, 312-939-5935

## SENIORS

- Home-Housing Opportunities & Maintenance for the Elderly, 773-252-3200
- Lincoln Park Senior Center, 312-943-6776
- Little Brothers Friends of the Elderly, 773-477-7702
- Senior Centers of Metropolitan Chicago Affiliate of Hull House Assoc., 773-525-3480

## WOMEN

- Chicago Abused Women Coalition, 773-278-4110
- Chicago Foundation for Women, 312-266-1176
- Chicago Metro Battered Women's Network, 312-360-1924
- Deborah's Place, 773-292-0707
- Sarah's Circle, 773-728-1991
- YWCA of Metropolitan Chicago, 312-372-6600

## YOUTH

- Alternatives, Inc., a multi-service youth agency, 773-973-5400
- Big Brothers/Big Sisters of Metropolitan Chicago, 312-427-0637
- Chicago Youth Centers, 312-648-1550
- Jobs for Youth/Chicago, 312-782-2086
- National Runaway Switchboard, 773-880-9860
- Youth Out Reach Services, 773-777-7112

## BY CAR

CHICAGO HAS FOUR MAJOR EXPRESSWAYS THAT EXTEND FROM THE city center like a minute hand reaching to 10 o'clock, 9 o'clock, 8 o'clock and 6 o'clock (on this clock, Lake Michigan would sit between Midnight and 5:30). During rush hour, you want to be anywhere *but* these thoroughfares.

**The Kennedy Expressway** (I-90; 10 o'clock) runs northwest to O'Hare International Airport and is reputed to be the busiest stretch of concrete in the country. Beyond O'Hare, I-90 (the Northwest Tollway in Illinois) will take you to Rockford and on up to Madison. For those who want a fast trip to the northern suburbs, take the Edens Expressway (North I-94), which splits from the Kennedy (or joins, depending upon the direction you're traveling) just north of the Irving Park Road ramps.

**The Eisenhower Expressway** (I-290; 9 o'clock) is your gateway to the western suburbs and the East-West toll road. As you leave the Loop on the Eisenhower, you will drive right through the U.S. Post Office, though expressway drive-thru postal service has still not been introduced.

**The Stevenson Expressway** (I-55; 8 o'clock) is the least crowded of Chicago's interstates. It's the route to Midway Airport, the western and southwestern suburbs, Joliet and Springfield.

**The Dan Ryan Expressway** (I-94; 6 o'clock) extends straight south and then splits at 95th Street either east to Indiana or as I-57 south-southwest toward Kankakee, Champaign-Urbana and ultimately, Memphis, Tennessee.

## TRAFFIC

Traffic congestion in Chicago is bad and getting worse. The traditional suburb-to-Chicago commute is still the grandaddy of all traffic jams, but the growing number of city-dwellers who work in the suburbs, and the even larger number of suburbanites who work in other suburbs, are changing the old rules. These days some of the worst congestion is not on the expressways within the city limits, but on those which link suburb to suburb. Many of these are older roads, which were not built to handle today's traffic volume.

The city has its own unique problems. Due to the gentrification of much of the North Side, the resultant increase in households with two or more cars, and the blossoming of strip malls and mega-stores, traffic and parking problems are now endemic. And it's just as bad on weekends. If you don't like sitting in a car for hours and getting nowhere, check out a convenient CTA train or bus line. Better yet, walk or take a bike. For more information on biking in the city, look in the "Sports & Recreation" chapter.

For a pleasant kind of driving excitement check out the justifiably famous view from Lake Shore Drive. The sight of the downtown at night, or shimmering in the light of dusk, can raise goose bumps on the arms of even the most jaded Chicagoans.

## POTHOLES AND WINTERIZING YOUR CAR

Due to the freezing winters, hot summers and heavy truck traffic, Chicago's streets are in below-average to generally poor condition. While you will spot work crews at nearly every block, the process of repairing the roads is an on-going and, to judge by the number of potholes, losing battle.

Make sure your car's suspension and tires are in good shape; around Halloween you should also "winterize" your vehicle. This involves checking and replacing all fluids including antifreeze and making sure the car's heater is in good condition. The *Chicago Sun-Times* publishes a guide to preparing your car for the season every year. Call 312-321-3000 to obtain a copy of the most recent supplement.

If you plan on buying a new car, many residents advise waiting until after the cruel winter, which can put beyond normal wear and tear on even the best made vehicle. When looking at a used car, consider the advantages of one from the suburbs or outlying areas, which may not have encountered as many hazards or hard usage as one driven in the city.

## CAR RENTAL

Chicago has car rental agencies throughout the city and suburbs. Call the following phone numbers for information, reservations and the nearest location.

- **AVIS,** 800-331-1212; O'Hare, 773-694-5600
- **Budget,** Chicago, 773-686-6800; suburbs, 630-968-6661
- **Enterprise,** in town, 800-736-8222; out of town, 800-325-8007
- **Hertz,** 800-654-3131; O'Hare, 773-686-7272
- **Rent-a-Wreck,** North and Downtown, 773-281-4242
  Many more car-rental agencies are listed in the Yellow Pages under "Automobile Rental."

## TAXIS

Taxis can be found at most hotels, transportation hubs such as Union Station and O'Hare International Airport and cruising the city's main thoroughfares. Step into the street and flag one down. However, away from these popular cab cruising areas you may have to wait a while to find a cab so if you're south of the South Loop, north of Wrigleyville and west of the Kennedy Expressway, you may want to call for a cab (although they don't always come when they say they will, especially if you're in an out of the way neighborhood).

## LIMOUSINES

Chicago has scores of limousine companies, many providing 24-hour service. Check the Yellow Pages under "Limousine."

## BY PUBLIC TRANSPORTATION

For all Chicago area transit information call the **RTA (Regional Transportation Authority)** Travel Information Center at 836-7000, using any Chicagoland area code; hearing impaired, 312-836-4949. RTA is the coordinator for all methods of public transportation — from CTA buses and "L" lines to suburban PACE buses and Metra trains. Call them with questions about fares, schedules, transfer options, etc., and to issue complaints, they are very helpful.

The **Chicago Transportation Authority (CTA)** includes all public transportation within city limits, except Metra. Their general information number is, 888-YOUR-CTA. A Chicago Transportation Authority map is an invaluable weapon in the battle against commuter confusion. You can get one at the Regional Transportation Authority Travel Information Center, 181 West Madison Street, at the CTA Main Offices, 312-664-7200, 222 Merchandise Mart Plaza, or during the summer at the City of

Chicago Information Booth on State Street.

Recently, the CTA introduced its new Transit Card. These can be purchased from the automatic card machines at any CTA station, at neighborhood currency exchanges or at Jewel and Dominick's food stores' customer-service counters. Transit Cards automatically keep track of how much fare credit you have. Each time you go through one of the automatic turnstiles (or farecard machines on the bus) the fare is deducted from your total and the card returned to you. An adult fare single trip costs $1.50 and a transfer (to another subway line or bus route within two hours of your original trip) will set you back 30¢. A second transfer (within the two hour time limit) is free. Transit Cards can be recharged with cash (machines accept change and $1, $2, $5, $10, and $20 bills) at any CTA station. There is also a bonus if you purchase enough fare credit; for every $13.50 you buy, you receive an additional $1.50 of fare credit.

Children under seven ride free. Seniors and youths are half price, including transfers, and during the school year, students ride at a reduced rate. The CTA also sells monthly passes, an unlimited monthly adult pass is $88.00. Just make sure your estimated weekly fares justify the expense.

As of this writing, the stations still have human fare-takers but there is a move afoot to eventually eliminate all such positions.

## THE "L"

The "L" is the quickest way to get around town, if it's going your way — and it usually is. There are five main lines that intersect in the Loop and extend like insect legs to all corners of the city. They are the Howard/Dan Ryan Red Line (north/south), the Lake/Englewood/Jackson Park Green Line (west/south), the O'Hare/Congress/Douglas Blue Line (west/northwest), the Ravenswood Brown Line (north/northwest) and the Midway Orange Line (southwest side and Midway Airport). If you're trying to get to either airport during rush hour, the Blue or Orange Lines are your fastest bet.

There also are two north suburban rapid-transit lines, the Evanston Express Purple Line and the Skokie Swift Yellow Line. Both trains run from the Howard station at the north end of the Howard/Dan Ryan Red line. The Skokie Swift runs directly west from the Howard station to the 4800 block, then continues north to just about Dempster (8800 North). The Evanston Express runs north, making eight stops in Evanston, ending at Linden. It runs express to and from the Loop during rush hour.

# BUSES

The CTA has bus routes running along most of Chicago's main arteries but not all lines have 24-hour service. (The CTA calls this "owl service" — look for it on the bus stop sign.) Exact fare of $1.50 or a transit card is required on buses.

# PACE

PACE, the suburban bus service, provides bus transportation through Chicago's suburbs. PACE tailors its routes and services to differing suburban areas. The types of service are: regular bus routes between suburban communities on a fixed route; local bus routes within a community; feeder bus routes providing morning and evening rush-hour service between residential areas and commuter train stations; and express routes providing direct service between suburbs and the Loop and between different suburbs. Exact fare of $1.50 or a transit card is required.

Schedules are available in village halls, libraries, from your bus driver and from the PACE office, 550 West Algonquin Road, Arlington Heights. To receive schedules by mail, call PACE at 847-364-813 or the RTA Travel Information Center, 836-7000, using any Chicagoland area code.

# METRA

Metra is the commuter railroad service that runs from the Loop to 225 suburban stations near and far. Service generally operates all day, including holidays; frequency varies in non-rush hour times from one to three hours. These trains have a fare system that is separate from the CTA. They also base their fares on the distance traveled. The following Metra lines leave from these stations:

- **Union Pacific,** North Western Station, 500 West Madison Street
- **Milwaukee District,** Union Station, 210 South Canal Street
- **Burlington Northern,** Union Station, 210 South Canal Street
- **Norfolk Southern,** Union Station, 210 South Canal Street
- **Heritage Corridor,** Union Station, 210 South Canal Street
- **Rock Island,** LaSalle Street Station, 414 South LaSalle Street
- **Metra Electric,** Randolph Street Station, 151 East Randolph Street
- **South Shore Line,** Randolph Street Station, 151 East Randolph Street

For information regarding Metra schedules, route and fares, call 312-322-6777. Printed schedules are available at all Metra stations and at the Metra Marketing Department, 547 West Jackson Boulevard, 312-322-6900 or 312-939-2929.

## AMTRAK

Amtrak, 800-USA-RAIL, provides inter-city rail service. Trains leave Union Station, 210 South Canal Street; there are stops at the Glenview, LaGrange and Naperville Metra stations. For affordable and efficient (yes!) service to such nearby cities as Detroit, Indianapolis, Milwaukee or St. Louis, Amtrak can't be beat. Amtrack's web site is *www.amtrak.com*.

# BY AIRLINE

**O'Hare International Airport**, 773-686-2200, with over 70 million passengers per year, is the busiest airport in the world. As you might expect, it can be crowded and confusing at times. O'Hare is the headquarters for United Airlines (the sparkling Terminal 1), and more than 50 other airlines have gates at one or more of O'Hare's five huge terminals. The airport is easy to get to via "L" or by car on the Kennedy (I-90). If you're driving, watch it during rush hour! You can miss a flight all too easily by underestimating travel time to O'Hare. If you're coming from downtown, the O'Hare/Congress/Douglas Blue Line will get you there the fastest. For drivers, there's plenty of short and long-term parking.

**Midway Airport**, 773-767-0500, is a square mile on the Southwest Side bounded by 55th Street and 63rd Street on the north and south, Cicero Avenue and Central Avenue on the east and west. Midway is served by the Stevenson Expressway (I-55) and is connected to the Loop by the CTA's new Midway rapid transit Orange Line. Once easily overshadowed by O'Hare, the growth of discount airlines such as Southwest, AIRTRAN, and Kiwi, who use Midway because of lower operating costs, has turned the older airport into a bustling commuter hub once again. Get there early if you need to park in the long-term lot (a shuttle bus will bring you to the terminal).

**Meigs Field**, 312-744-4787, is an embattled single runway on landfill extending south from Shedd Aquarium that was created for Chicago's 1933 Century of Progress Exposition. It's generally used by private planes filled with government officials and business people who want to get in and out of the Loop quickly. It's also where Mayor Daley wants to erect a new lakefront park; as a result, it may not be long for this world.

THERE ARE HUNDREDS OF HOTELS AND MOTELS IN CHICAGO, ranging from the bare bones room-with-a-bed motel to luxurious hotel suites with breathtaking views of Lake Michigan and the Chicago skyline. Always remember to ask the hotel reservationist about discounts or weekend packages. Many lodgings have daily, unadvertised specials only offered if you inquire. If you need a room in a hurry, call **Hot Rooms,** 773-468-7666, a hotel-reservation service that will help you reserve a room at special discount rates.

Keep in mind that room rates vary by the season (off season begins January 1 and ends March 31) and by the convention (no discounts during large events like the National Restaurant Convention which occurs in the last week in May). If you're looking for a babysitter for the kids, check with the front desk to see if the hotel provides that service. If not, call the **American Registry for Nurses and Sitters,** 773-248-8100 and they can arrange to have a babysitter come to your hotel. (Look in the "Child Care" chapter under "Babysitting" for more information.)

The following list of hotels and motels is by no means complete. With an eye to your pocketbook, we have shied away from most of the expensive hotels in favor of more reasonably priced accommodations in good locations. If you are just passing through O'Hare, try one of the more than 20 or so hotels around the airport, starting with the OHare Hilton across from Terminal 2 (773-686-8000). For a more complete listing, you can call the **Hotel and Motel Association of Illinois,** 312-236-3473, or check the Yellow Pages under "Hotels and Motels." Another good source for hotel and motel recommendation are AAA travel guides. Free to members, their listings are useful because AAA weeds out those hotels which are not up to their standards. Finally, **Quikbook** is a discount room reservation service which costs nothing to join and offers reduced room rates for many hotels. For a list of cities and hotels and information about them, visit their website at *www.quikbook.com* or call 800-789-9887.

## INEXPENSIVE LODGINGS

- **Best Western-Grant Park**, 1100 South Michigan Avenue, 312-922-2900; room prices range from $99 to $128 a night.
- **City Suites**, 933 West Belmont Avenue, 773-404-3400; room prices are $109 a night.
- **Comfort Inn**, 601 West Diversey Parkway, 773-348-2810; room prices range from $109 to $205 a night.
- **Days Inn - Gold Coast**, 1816 North Clark Street, 312-664-3040; room prices from $85 to $135 a night.
- **Days Inn - Near North**, 644 West Diversey Parkway, 773-525-7010; room prices range from $74 to $104 a night.
- **Heart of Chicago Motel**, 5990 North Ridge Avenue, 773-271-9181; room prices start at $50.
- **HOJO Inn**, 720 North LaSalle Street, 312-664-8100; room prices range from $78 to $95 a night.
- **Ohio House Motel**, 600 North LaSalle Street, 312-943-6000; room prices are $78 a night.
- **Surf Hotel**, 555 West Surf Street, 773-528-8400; room prices are $79 to $109 a night.

## MIDDLE-RANGE LODGINGS

- **Best Western Inn of Chicago**, 162 East Ohio Street, 312-787-3100; rooms start at $109 to $169 per night, but ask about weekend package rates for rooms offered at $79-$85 a night.
- **Days Inn-Lakeshore**, 644 North Lake Shore Drive, 312-943-9200; room prices range from $109 to $184 a night.
- **Omni Orrington Hotel**, 1710 Orrington Avenue, Evanston, 847-866-8700; room prices range from $145 to $165 a night.
- **Ramada Inn Lake Shore**, 4900 South Lake Shore Drive, 773-288-5800; room prices range from $89 to $99 a night.
- **The Seneca**, 200 East Chestnut Street, 312-988-4405; room prices range from $139 to $269 a night.

## LUXURY LODGINGS

- **Four Seasons Hotel**, 120 East Delaware Place, 312-280-8800; recently rated the number one hotel in the world in a *Condé Nast Travelers* reader's survey. Room prices range from $330 to $445. Ask about weekend package rates which start at $270 a night.

- **Westin - River North**, 312-320 North Dearborn Street, 312-744-1900; room prices range from $285 to $315 a night. Ask about weekend and special rates which start at $179 a night.

## HOSTELS

- **Chicago International Hostel**, 6318 North Winthrop Avenue, 773-262-1011; rates are $13 a night. The hostel offers dormitory style living, four to eight beds per room with showers, with a full kitchen. There is a late curfew.
- **International House of Chicago**, 1414 East 59th Street, 773-753-2270; rates are $36 per night ($16 for members of American Youth Hostels or AYH) for a single room with a shared bath. Part of the University of Chicago's Housing Department, the hostel has a cafeteria nearby and is open 24 hours.

## BED & BREAKFAST

- **B & B Midwest Reservations**, guest rooms in suburban Chicago and northern Indiana, 800-342-2632.
- **Bed & Breakfast Chicago Inc.**, 312-951-0085, offers apartments, rooms and homes in more than 80 Chicago area locations.
- **Heritage Bed & Breakfast Registry**, 800-431-554, offers hosted and unhosted accommodations in Chicago (mostly North Side) homes.
- **Villa Toscana Guest House**, 3447 Halsted, 773-404-2643. Great North Side location; surprisingly quiet and reasonably priced.

## SUMMER ONLY

**Northwestern University's** Chicago campus, 312-503-8514, offers rooms to non-students for summer occupancy. Call well in advance. Rooms cost from $15 to $21 per night, depending upon the dormitory and room location. Specify your reasons for wanting summer accommodations when you ask for an application.

Northwestern University's main campus in Evanston does not provide summer dormitory accommodations for non-students. However, the Housing Department, 847-491-3741, does provide information on summer sublet or apartment-to-share information. You might also check with the fraternities and sororities for short-term housing in their houses.

You can also call **DePaul University Housing**, 312-362-8000 or **Loyola University Housing**, 773-274-3000, to check on availability.

## WEEKLY LEASES

- **Extended Stay America**, 800-398-7829, has locations in Rolling Meadows, Gurnee, Downers Grove, Waukegan and Itasca. A room with a queen-size bed, kitchenette, utensils and weekly maid service ranges from $250-$320.

## MONTHLY LEASES

- **Doral Michigan Avenue,** 151 North Michigan Avenue, 312- 616-6005, offers furnished apartments for a minimum 30 day stay. The lease includes cable television, kitchen amenities, health-club memberships, linens and weekly maid service. Furnished "corporate suites" start at $1,700 per month for a studio, $2,000 for a one-bedroom, $2,700 for a two-bedroom; discounts are available for stays of three months or more. Unfurnished apartments can also be had for significantly lower rates, although a one-year lease is required.
- You can also try **Delaware Towers**, 25 East Delaware Place, 312-944-4245. A "small room or studio" goes for $79, a one-bedroom costs $125, includes cable TV but no health club. Monthly rates available.
- **Oakwood Corporate Housing**, 312-642-0120, has 12 fully furnished apartments with cable TV, pool and gym and weekly maid service. Rates range from $2,100 - $2,300 per month.

## TRANSIENT YMCAS

- **Lawson YMCA**, 30 West Chicago Avenue, 312-944-6211, will charge $80 for a three-day stay ($25 per night plus a $5 key deposit), after which time you will have to talk to the manager about staying on. Rates are $72.50 per week and $268 a month for individual rooms containing a desk, chair, twin bed, closet, sink and mirror; there is a community bath.
- **The Lincoln-Belmont YMCA**, 3333 North Marshfield Avenue, 773-248-3333, is a men-only residential Y offering rock-bottom prices on rooms for rent by the week or the month. For $64-$80 per week or $269-$373 per month you get a bed, desk, chair, closet and ceiling fan. A $10 background check is required.

CONTRARY TO WHAT A NEW ARRIVAL MAY BELIEVE, NOT ALL OF Illinois is flat or filled with cornfields; to the west lie rolling hills and the beautiful Mississippi River valley; to the north, wooded lakelands and, to the south, historical Indian lands and state parks.

A car makes getting to any of the following places a breeze. Amtrak is an option to places like Springfield or Milwaukee. Most of the following suggestions are perfect for a long day trip, although bed and breakfasts abound for those who choose to spend the night.

Legalized gambling, a relatively new development in the state, has sprung up on riverboat casinos along the Ohio and Mississippi Rivers as well as parts of Lake Michigan (see the "Sports and Recreation" chapter of this book). Call the **Illinois Department of Tourism** at 800-223-0121, for more information.

## GALENA

A living history book with 85 percent of its buildings included in the National Historic Register, Galena, lying three hours to the west, is also the hometown of Ulysses S. Grant. Grant's house, presented to him by the community upon his triumphant return from the Civil War, is only one of the charms of this beautiful town located on the Mississippi River. The nearby Eagle Ridge resort is a golfer's paradise, set in the hills with numerous courses. Call the Galena Tourism Information Center, 800-747-9377 for more information.

## INDIANA DUNES STATE PARK

Forty-five minutes south of Chicago on the Indiana shore of Lake Michigan (near the city of Chesterton), Indiana Dunes State Park is a popular spot for summertime beach-goers. The over 2,000 acre park boasts plenty of picnic spots, campgrounds (reservations must be made in advance for Memorial or Labor Day weekends) and, of course, sand dunes. For park information, call 219-926-1952 or the Indiana Department of Tourism, 800-289-6646.

## LAKE GENEVA

Less then two hours north just across the Illinois/Wisconsin border, lovely Lake Geneva has been a favorite getaway for Chicagoans for generations. A stroll around part of the lake to admire the huge mansions built by wealthy vacationers years past, water-skiing, fishing and antique-hunting are just a few of the ways you can spend the day. For more information call the Wisconsin Department of Tourism, 800-372-2737.

## MILWAUKEE

Two hours north of Chicago and past Gurnee (home of Gurnee Mills, a huge outlet mall also worth a visit if you're a shopaholic), Milwaukee has been called a smaller version of Chicago. Its Central European heritage means there's plenty of lively taverns, restaurants, interesting neighbor-hoods, and of course, breweries. Call the Milwaukee Convention and Tourism Bureau, 414-273-3950 for more details.

## SPRINGFIELD

Home of Abraham Lincoln as well as dozens of historical buildings, the state capital also hosts the Illinois State Fair every August. A long drive (around four hours) and best for a weekend trip. Call the Springfield Convention and Visitor's Bureau, 800-545-7300. For state fair informa-tion, call 800-545-7300.

## STARVED ROCK STATE PARK

A mere two hours west of Chicago, the 19 canyons that make up this state park include natural attractions such as waterfalls, 600 types of wild-flowers and incredible views. A good spot for camping, fishing or boat-ing, the park is also worth a visit in the winter months for viewing frozen waterfalls, ice skating or cross-country skiing. For more information call 815-667-4906 or the Starved Rock Lodge and Conference Center, 815-667-4211.

## JANUARY

- **Chicago Cubs Convention**
- **Twelfth Night Festival,** Pleasant Home
- **Chicago Boat, Sports & RV Show,** McCormick Place

## FEBRUARY

- **African American History Month,** Chicago Cultural Center
- **Chinese New Year Festival,** Chinatown (Cermak Road and Wentworth Avenue)
- **University of Chicago Folk Festival,** Hyde Park
- **Winter Break Festival,** Chicago Cultural Center

## MARCH

- **St. Patrick's Day Parade,** Dearborn Street and Wacker Drive
- **Chicago Flower and Garden Show,** Navy Pier
- **Spring Dog Show,** McCormick Place
- **Winnetka Antiques Show,** Winnetka Community House

## APRIL

- **Cheney Mansion Antique Show,** Oak Park
- **Chicago Latino Film Festival**

## MAY

- **Cinco De Mayo,** Douglas Park
- **Chicago International Art Exposition,** Lakefront
- **International Theater Festival,** (various locations)

## JUNE

- **Chicago Blues Festival,** Grant Park
- **Gay & Lesbian Pride Parade,** Wrigleyville/Lakeview
- **Gospel Festival,** Grant Park
- **Hyde Park Art Fair,** Hyde Park
- **Midsommarfest,** Andersonville
- **Old Town Art Fair,** Lincoln Park West and Orleans Street at Menomonee Street
- **Printer's Row Book Fair,** Printer's Row
- **Taste of Chicago,** Grant Park

## JULY

- **Taste of Chicago** (continued), Grant Park
- **Fiesta del Sol,** Pilsen
- **Fourth of July Celebration,** Grant Park
- **Chicago Park District Air and Water Show,** Grant Park

## AUGUST

- **Air and Water Show,** Lakefront at Grant Park
- **Bucktown Arts Fest,** Bucktown
- **Fiesta del Sol,** Pilsen
- **Jazzfest, South Shore Cultural Center,** 71st Street and South Shore Drive
- **Gold Coast Art Fair,** Gold Coast
- **Summer Fest West,** Garfield Park
- **Venetian Night,** Lakefront at Grant Park

## SEPTEMBER

- **Around the Coyote,** Wicker Park/Bucktown
- **German-American Fest,** Lincoln Square
- **Jazz Festival,** Grant Park
- **Mexican Independence Day Parade,** Dearborn and Wacker Drive
- **Labor Day Parade,** Dearborn and Wacker Drive
- **Taste of Romania,** St. Alphonsus Church
- **Viva! Chicago Latin Music Festival,** Grant Park

## OCTOBER

- **Chicago Marathon**
- **Columbus Day Parade**, Dearborn and Wacker Drive
- **Old Town Haunted House**, 226 West Schiller Street

## NOVEMBER

- **Veteran's Day Parade**, Dearborn Street and Wacker Drive
- **Brach's Holiday Parade**, Michigan Avenue
- **Michigan Avenue Festival of Lights**, Michigan Avenue

## DECEMBER

- **Christmas Tours of Frank Lloyd Wright Home and Studio**, Oak Park
- **Julmark nad (Christmasfest)**, Swedish American Museum Center
- **Kiddie New Year**, Shedd Aquarium

*Call 911 for police, fire and ambulance emergencies.*

## ALCOHOL

Alcohol, Drug & Abuse Helpline, 800-234-0420
Alcoholics Anonymous, 312-346-1475
Alcoholism and Substance Abuse, 312-988-7900
United Way Community Information and Referral, 312-876-0010

## ANIMALS

Animal bites, 911
Animal Control Center, 312-744-5000
Animal Welfare League, 773-667-0088
Anti-Cruelty Society, 312-644-8338
Dead Animal Removal (Mayor's Office), 312-744-5000
Dog License (City Clerk), 312-744-6875
Tree House, 312-784-5488

## AUTOMOBILES

Abandoned Car (Mayor's Office), 312-744-5000
Illinois Secretary of State, 312-814-2262, 217-782-7880

## BIRTH AND DEATH CERTIFICATES

Cook County, 312-443-7790

## CITY OF CHICAGO

Emergency Services, 312-747-7247
Mayor's Office, 312-744-4000, 312-744-5000

## CHILD ABUSE AND NEGLECT

Emergency Services, 312-747-7247
Illinois Child Abuse Hotline, 800-252-2873
Parental Stress Services, 312-372-7368
United Way Community Information & Referral Services, 312-876-0010

## CONSUMER COMPLAINTS AND SERVICES

Attorney General, Consumer Fraud Division, 312-814-3000
Better Business Bureau of Chicago, complaints only, 312-832-0500
Chicago Department of Consumer Services, 312-744-9400
Citizens' Utility Board (C.U.B.), 800-669-5556
Consumer Affairs Division of the Illinois Commerce Commission, 312-814-2887
Mayor's Office, 312-744-4000, 312-744-5000
State's Attorney, Consumer Division, 312-345-2400

## CRIME

Crime in Progress, 911
Emergency Services, 312-747-7247
Report Crime in Your Neighborhood, 312-372-0101

## CRISIS HOTLINES

Alcoholism and Substance Abuse, 312-988-7900
Drug Care, St. Elizabeth's Hospital, 773-278-5015
Gamblers Anonymous, 312-346-1588
Narcotics Anonymous, 708-848-4884
Runaway Switchboard, 800-621-4000

## DENTAL EMERGENCY SERVICE

Chicago Dental Referral Service, 312-836-7305

## ELECTED OFFICIALS & GOVERNMENT

Chicago Ward Aldermanic Information, 312-744-3081
City of Chicago Board of Elections, 312-269-7900

Citizens Information Service, 312-939-4636
Mayor's Office, 312-744-4000, 312-744-5000
Cook County Board of Elections, 312-443-5150
Social Security, 800-772-1213
Governor's Office, 312-814-2121

## ENTERTAINMENT

Chicago Live Concert (contemporary music), 312-666-6667
Chicago Music Alliance (opera & classical), 312-987-9296
Chicago Music Hotline (classical), 312-987-1123
Dance Hotline, 312-419-8383
Mayor's Office of Special Events, 312-744-3315
Theater Tickets by phone, Hot Tixx, 312-975-1755
Ticketmaster, 312-559-1212

## HOUSING

Chicago Department of Housing, 773-285-5800
Complaints, City of Chicago Department of Inspectional Services,
312-747-1500
Illinois Tenants Union, 773-478-1133
Mayor's Office, 312-744-4000, 312-744-5000

## INCOME TAX

Federal, 800-829-3676
Illinois, 800-732-8866

## LIBRARY

Des Plaines Public Library, 847-827-5551
Evanston Public Library, 847-866-0300
Harold Washington Library (the "main" library), 312-747-4300
Oak Park Main Library, 708-383-8200
Skokie Public Library, 847-673-7774
Wilmette Public Library, 847-256-5025

## PARK DISTRICTS

Chicago, 312-747-2200

*(PARK DISTRICTS continued)*
    Deerfield, 847-945-0650
    Des Plaines, 847-391-5700
    Evanston, 847-866-2910
    Northbrook, 847-291-2960
    Oak Park, 708-383-0002
    Rosemont, 847-823-6685
    Skokie, 847-674-1500
    Wilmette, 847-256-6100

## PARKING

City Clerk's Office (City Stickers), 312-744-6861
Oak Park Village Parking Department, 708-383-6400, ext.,236
Parking Ticket Inquiries, 312-744-7275

## POST OFFICE

City of Chicago, main, 312-654-3788, complaints, 312-983-8400
Deerfield, 847-945-0257
Des Plaines, 847-827-5591
Evanston, 847-328-6201
Northbrook, 847-272-0018
Oak Park, 708-848-7900
Skokie, 847-676-2200
Wilmette, 847-251-8644

## RAPE

Emergency Assistance, 911
Sexual Assault Hotline, 888-293-2080

## SANITATION AND GARBAGE

Chicago Department of Streets and Sanitation, 312-744-5000

## SHIPPING

FedEx, 800-463-3339
UPS, 800-742-5877

## SPORTS

Bears, 847-615-2327
Blackhawks, 312-455-7000
Bulls, 312-455-4000
Cubs, 773-404-2827
Fire, 888-MLS-FIRE
White Sox, 312-674-1000
Wolves, 847-390-0404

## TAXIS

Checker Cabs, 312-243-2537
Dart Cab Co., 773-866-9200
Flash Cab Co., 773-561-1444
Jiffy Cab Co., 773-487-9000
Yellow Cab Co., 312-829-4222

## TIME

773-976-8463 (toll call; 50¢)

## TOURISM

Chicago Architecture Foundation, 312-922-3432
Chicago Office of Tourism, 312-744-2400
Illinois Department of Tourism, 800-487-2446

## TRAFFIC INFORMATION, REPORTS AND DIRECTIONS

D-R-I-V-E-6-7

## TRAFFIC TICKETS

12-744-6146

# TRANSPORTATION

## AIRPORTS

O'Hare International Airport Information, 773-686-2200
Midway Airport Information, 773-767-0500
Meigs Field Information, 312-744-4787

## AMTRAK

800-USA-RAIL

## REGIONAL TRANSPORTATION AUTHORITY (RTA)

CTA, 888-YOUR-CTA
Metra, 312-322-6777
PACE, 847-364-8130
RTA Travel Information, 836-7000, using any Chicagoland area code

## UTILITIES

Electric wires down or other electrical emergencies, ComEd, 800-334-7661
Gas leaks, Peoples Gas Customer Service, 312-240-7000
Telephone Repair Service, 888-611-4466
Water main leaks, Chicago Department of Water, 312-744-7038

## WEATHER

773-976-2200 (toll call; 75¢)

## ZIP CODE INFORMATION

312-654-3895

# A CHICAGO READING LIST

*American Insitute of Architects Guide to Chicago*, ALICE SINKEVITCH, EDITOR.
If you like modern architecture, this is the city, and this is the book.

*Boss* BY MIKE ROYKO.
The seminal book on post-WW II Chicago politics.

*The Chicago Tenant Handbook* BY ED SACHS
Worth the price of ten lawyers. No unhappy Chicago renter should be without it.

*The Jungle* BY UPTON SINCLAIR
Magnificently readable and important turn-of-the-century diatribe against unrestrained capitalism. Takes you back to Chicago of one hundred years ago.

*Lost Chicago* BY DAVID LOWE
After the Chicago Fire of 1871, architects from around the country came to Chicago to help rebuild it. This book chronicles those great edifices which later fell to the wrecking ball to make room for the steel-and-glass skyscrapers of today.

*The Man With the Golden Arm* BY NELSON ALGREN
The now trendy Bucktown and Wicker Park neighborhoods were once Chicago's mean streets and Algren their poet-laureate. Here's a look.

*Nature's Metropolis: Chicago and the Great West* BY BILL CRONON
A fascinating book explaining how and why Chicago became the Second City.

*Zagat Survey, Chicago Restaurants.*
If you love to eat out, you've come to the right town. Get the Chicago edition of this great restaurant series. Updated annually.

**M**ark Wukas is a longtime Chicago journalist and freelance writer. He has worked for United Press International, the City News Bureau and *The Regional News* in Palos Heights and his work appears regularly in the *Chicago Tribune.* A native South Sider, he is a student of Chicago history and neighborhoods. Wukas also is an adjunct faculty member in the Fiction Writing Department at Columbia College. He has both an M.A. and B.A. in English from the University of Illinois at Urbana-Champaign.

**T**hor Ringler is a poet whose work has appeared in numerous obscure literary journals. This book is his first opportunity to reach an audience of more than fifty. Currently he works in advertising, though he has held a variety of jobs: waiter, carpenter, cook, baker, clock repairman, teacher. He has an M.F.A. from the University of Pittsburgh and performs his work frequently in the Chicago area.

# READER RESPONSE FORM

We would appreciate your comments regarding the *Newcomer's Handbook™ for Chicago*. If you've found any mistakes or omissions or if you would just like to express your opinion about the guide, please let us know. We will consider any suggestions in our next edition, and if we use your comments, we'll send you a *free* copy of our next edition. Send this response form to:

Reader Response Department
First Books, Inc.
P.O. Box 578147
Chicago, IL 60657

Comments:

_____

_____

_____

_____

_____

_____

_____

_____

_____

Name: _____

Address _____

_____

_____

Telephone (          ) _____

P.O. Box 578147
Chicago, IL 60657
(773) 276-5911
www.firstbooks.com

# NEWCOMER'S ORDER FORM HANDBOOK ™

## THE ORIGINAL, ALWAYS UPDATED, ABSOLUTELY INVALUABLE GUIDES FOR PEOPLE MOVING TO A CITY!

*Find out about neigborhoods, apartment and house hunting, money matters, deposits/leases, getting settled, helpful services, shopping for the home, places of worship, cultural life, sports/recreation, vounteering, green space, transportation, temporary lodgings and useful telephone numbers!*

|  | # COPIES | TOTAL |
|---|---|---|
| Newcomer's Handbook™ for Atlanta | _____ x $13.95 | $_____ |
| Newcomer's Handbook™ for Boston | _____ x $13.95 | $_____ |
| Newcomer's Handbook™ for Chicago | _____ x $14.95 | $_____ |
| Newcomer's Handbook™ for Los Angeles | _____ x $13.95 | $_____ |
| Newcomer's Handbook™ for Minneapolis-St. Paul | _____ x $14.95 | $_____ |
| Newcomer's Handbook™ for New York City | _____ x $17.95 | $_____ |
| Newcomer's Handbook™ for San Francisco | _____ x $13.95 | $_____ |
| Newcomer's Handbook™ for Seattle | _____ x $13.95 | $_____ |
| Newcomer's Handbook™ for Washington D.C. | _____ x $13.95 | $_____ |
| **SUBTOTAL** | | $_____ |
| **TAX** (*IL residents add 8.75% sales tax*) | | $_____ |
| **POSTAGE & HANDLING** (*$4.00 first book, $.75 each add'l*) | | $_____ |
| **TOTAL** | | $_____ |

**SHIP TO:**

Name _____

Title _____

Company _____   _____

Address _____

City _____ State _____ Zip _____

Phone Number ( ) _____

Send this order form and a check or money order payable to:
First Books, Inc.

First Books, Inc., Mail Order Department
P.O. Box 578147, Chicago, IL 60657
773-276-5911

*Allow 2 weeks for delivery*

# CTA "L" MAP

travel information phone 312-836-7000. CTA Web site: http://www.transitchicago.com

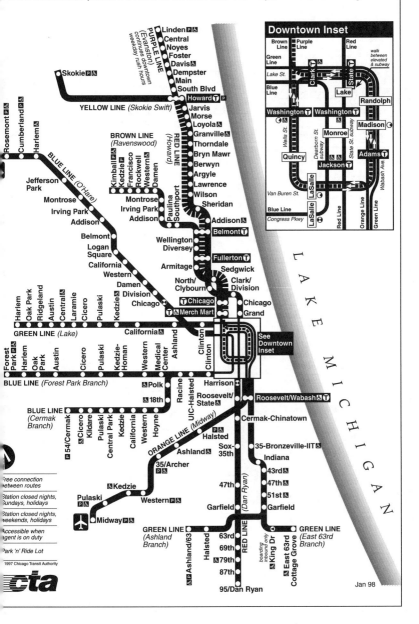

## Downtown Inset

| Brown Line | Purple Line |
| Green Line | |
| Blue Line | |

Lake St.

Clark

State

walk between elevated & subway

Lake

Randolph

Washington

Washington

Madison

Wells St.

Monroe

Dearborn St. subway

State St. subway

Quincy

Jackson

Adams

Van Buren St.

Blue Line

Congress Pkwy

LaSalle

LaSalle

Red Line

Orange Line

Green Line

Wabash Ave.

**PURPLE LINE** *(Evanston) continues downtown weekday rush hours*

- Linden
- Central
- Noyes
- Foster
- Davis
- Dempster
- Main
- South Blvd
- Howard

**YELLOW LINE** *(Skokie Swift)*

Skokie

**BROWN LINE** *(Ravensworth)*

- Kimball
- Kedzie
- Francisco
- Rockwell
- Western
- Damen

**RED LINE** *(Howard)*

- Jarvis
- Morse
- Loyola
- Granville
- Thorndale
- Bryn Mawr
- Berwyn
- Argyle
- Lawrence
- Wilson
- Sheridan
- Addison
- Belmont
- Wellington
- Diversey
- Fullerton
- Sedgwick
- Clark/Division
- Chicago
- Grand

Rosemont

Cumberland

Harlem

**BLUE LINE** *(O'Hare)*

Jefferson Park

Montrose

Irving Park

Addison

Belmont

Logan Square

California

Western

Damen

Division

Chicago

Montrose

Irving Park

Addison

Paulina

Southport

Montrose

Wellington

Diversey

Armitage

North/Clybourn

Chicago

Merch Mart

See Downtown Inset

**GREEN LINE** *(Lake)*

- Harlem
- Oak Park
- Ridgeland
- Austin
- Central
- Laramie
- Cicero
- Pulaski
- Kedzie
- California
- Ashland
- Clinton

**BLUE LINE** *(Forest Park Branch)*

- Forest Park
- Harlem
- Oak Park
- Austin
- Cicero
- Kedzie-Homan
- Western
- Medical Center
- Clinton
- Polk
- 18th

**BLUE LINE** *(Cermak Branch)*

- 54/Cermak
- Cicero
- Kildare
- Pulaski
- Central Park
- Kedzie
- California
- Western
- Hoyne
- Racine
- UIC-Halsted

Harrison

Roosevelt/State

Roosevelt/Wabash

Cermak-Chinatown

**ORANGE LINE** *(Midway)*

- Halsted
- Ashland
- 35/Archer
- Kedzie
- Pulaski
- Western
- Midway

**Free connection between routes**

**Station closed nights, Sundays, holidays**

**Station closed nights, weekends, holidays**

**Accessible when agent is on duty**

**Park 'n' Ride Lot**

1997 Chicago Transit Authority

cta

- Sox-35th
- 35-Bronzeville-IIT
- Indiana
- 43rd
- 47th
- 51st
- Garfield

**RED LINE** *(Dan Ryan)*

**GREEN LINE** *(Ashland Branch)*

- Ashland/63
- Halsted
- 63rd
- 69th
- 79th
- 87th
- 95/Dan Ryan

47th

Garfield

boarding inbound only

King Dr

**GREEN LINE** *(East 63rd Branch)*

- East 63rd
- Cottage Grove

LAKE MICHIGAN

Jan 98

# NOTES